PAUL SH

A Question
of Healing

The Failure of Christian Healing?
An examination of the results of Christian
healing ministries today in the light of their
beliefs and practices

malcolm down
PUBLISHING

First published 2022 by Malcolm Down Publishing Ltd
www.malcolmdown.co.uk
Registered Office: Welwyn Garden City, England

British Library Cataloguing-in-Publication Data
A catalogue record for this book is available from the British Library.

ISBN 978-1-915046-20-8

Cover design by Esther Kotecha
Art direction by Sarah Grace

Contents

⚬————◁ ◦ ▷————⚬

Introduction

Context

What is it that inspires one to write a book about healing? There are several major influences associated with this work. Firstly, there is the local church influence. The church that the author first belonged to was not strong in the ministry of Christian healing. However, when, as a young married couple, he and his wife were led to look for a new church, they joined West Church in Bangor, County Down.

For those who are unfamiliar with Northern Ireland's church history, Bangor was a major ecclesiastical centre in the 5th, 6th and 7th centuries, producing church leaders such as Saint Gall, Saint Comgall, Saint Colmcille and Saint Columbanus. The monks at Bangor Abbey were known to have taken their turn to engage in uninterrupted prayer and worship for a period of 150 years, creating an early 24/7 prayer movement, and Bangor was a primary centre from which missionaries were sent and from which much of mainland Europe was evangelised. Brutal Viking attacks brought this era to a sudden and bloody halt. Nevertheless, the influence has continued and the town's annual Worldwide Missionary Convention is still one of the best-attended Christian events in Northern Ireland. The West Church congregation (commonly known simply as 'West') is a Presbyterian church, planted from one of the town-centre churches to service the growing community on the outskirts of Bangor to the west, which has resulted from new housing developments. The late David Bailie was appointed as minister for the new congregation, shortly after he had returned from India, and it grew moderately from the transfer of members of other churches as they moved to these newly created housing developments. Then came an event that changed everything: the visit of Revd Tom Smail, a Church of Scotland minister. Tom had received an empowerment that David Bailie recognised as something that he didn't have, and at the end of a weekend of special meetings, Tom asked David if he could pray with him for an infilling of the Holy Spirit. In a written testimony (available on request at West), David told the story:

> I didn't feel much and told him [Tom] so, but he encouraged me to believe. And his faith in Christ's faithfulness was justified. After a week struggling with unbelief, I came to experience that the Holy Spirit was working in and through me in a new way. Not only was I given a 'new' Bible, a new dimension in prayer and praise, a new awareness of the Holy Spirit within, but I found that people for whom I prayed were clearly filled with the Spirit; some received healing. One day, when I was praying in my study, I found myself doing something that I had never seen anyone else do. I raised my arms instinctively in worship to God, and then began to praise Him fluently, and with great spiritual release and joy, in a new language.

Changes began to take place gradually, almost unobtrusively. I remember, for example, visiting a home where a lady, who suffered quite severely from arthritis, had just returned from the Royal Victoria Hospital, where she had been given a gloomy prognosis. She and her husband were deeply upset. I remember saying, from an impulse of sympathy and compassion, 'Let us pray.' I found myself, spontaneously, resting my hand upon her shoulder – something that I would not normally have done. In my mind, I was not thinking that I was laying my hands upon her for healing. That was not in my mind at all. Now the next day, she was able to walk with ease, more than a mile into Bangor and out again.

Another lady I visited was in great pain with what turned out to be a cancer from which she was expected to suffer a great deal. Through the prayer, her pain left entirely and she was filled with a peace passing all understanding. Her pain never returned, and though she was called on to be with the Lord, her 'sickroom' was so filled with the peace and joy of the Lord that everyone who entered experienced it.

The result was significant, leading not only to the minister of the congregation but also to many of the newly appointed elders receiving this baptism. Consequently, spiritual gifts such as speaking in tongues, words of knowledge and healing were commonplace in West long before the author joined. The weekly healing service was well known and was attended by individuals from various denominational affiliations and a wide geographical radius. This service is mentioned in relation to the healing of Brian Scott later in this work.

The author has had several healing touches in West himself; one in 1993 when a visiting speaker, the late Revd Jimmy Smith from Georgia, USA, was ministering. The following year, the Revd John Coles and his wife Anne, who had been greatly influenced in Toronto by what came to be known as the 'Toronto Blessing', were invited for a weekend of special meetings. John went on to be Director of New Wine from 2001 to 2014 but, on the occasion of his visit to West, he brought a signs-and-wonders ministry that also included healing.

Secondly, the author is interested in what is happening in other parts of the world. If there are phenomena associated with church meetings and ministry in other regions, particularly if revival is operating in some measure, it is natural to have a hunger for such things. The author had read with zeal the accounts of the impact that Northern Ireland's 1859 revival and the Hebrides Revival, with which Duncan Campbell was associated, had each made on their respective local communities. During the course of this work, the author also makes several references to experiences and individuals associated with Cali, Colombia, with which he has made a particular connection. The author was first drawn to this South American city through an incredible video documentary called *Transformations*, produced by the Sentinel Group. Sentinel is a community of researchers, film-makers and ministers dedicated to the task of preparing needy communities for spiritual revival and societal transformation.[1] It was founded in 1990 by George Otis, Jr. Otis, after working in 'frontier' evangelisation efforts for many years, became concerned about what he recognised as spiritual oppression and its persistence. His investigation into this problem took him to more than fifty nations. As a result of his investigations, Otis presented in *Transformations* his first synopsis of four distinctly different that had experienced significant transformation as a result of deliberate spiritual action taken by the churches at their heart. Cali was one of those communities where, as a result of corporate prayer, an entire drugs cartel was defeated almost without a fight. Several years later, the author had the opportunity to visit Cali. It was on that first trip that he met Pastor Hendrik Hoere, a Dutch missionary who had been ministering in Cali since the 1980s. He had been the junior pastor to Julio Ruibal, the pastor who had been shot prior to the Cali revival and whose death had united the members of the Cali Pastors' Association. The author has learned much from Hendrik in the realms of revival and operating in the supernatural.

Thirdly, there are a number of personal friends whose lives are all about the Christian healing ministry. Paul Bennison is one such individual who has travelled to more than a hundred countries in a role that can be best described as that of a 'healing evangelist'. The author has ministered with Paul on many occasions and refers to some of the resulting experiences herein. Paul has enough stories to fill many volumes, of which several are truly miraculous and apostolic in their nature. However, there are a number of references to his experiences made in this work.

---

1. https://www.sentinelgroup.org/about (accessed 7 February 2022).

Fourthly, there is the Belfast-based organisation Divine Healing Ministries – founded by Brother David Jardine[2] and now led by Fergus McMorrow – with which the author and his wife have had a long association.

The fifth reason for the author's wanting to write this book is the influence of Union Theological College in Belfast, where his growing interest in this subject led him to study it at the level of a Master's degree. It is from this period of study that the more scholarly content of the work emanates.

The Problem

The problem with contemporary Christian healing is that it is seen in general as being a failure, firstly by opponents of the Christian faith, particularly atheists, who use the fact of failure in many instances to ridicule the Church and the God of the Bible. Secondly, as proof of their belief, by opponents of the theology that God can and does act supernaturally in the realm of physical healing in this present Church age. These opponents cite many instances where supernatural gifts are claimed to be in operation, individuals are declared healed, yet their illnesses do not abate and, in some cases, worsen. This represents, according to the latter group of opponents, the failure of those engaged in such a ministry to recognise that their healing ministry is unbiblical and therefore futile. Keith Warrington is a contemporary writer

---

2. Along with a group of like-minded Christians, Brother David Jardine founded Interdenominational Divine Healing Ministries in 1992. Since then, they have been praying for the healing of individuals and of our land (Northern Ireland). Brother Jardine is an ordained Church of Ireland clergyman and also a member of the Society of St Francis, a religious community in the Anglican Church. He was a chaplain at Crumlin Road Prison, Belfast (1975–1985). From 1985 to 1988, he worked in two churches in New York. Brother David has led the formation of an extensive team of trained healers, who by invitation have attended many churches and associated venues throughout Ireland. See http://www.divinehealingministries.org/Brother-David.aspx (accessed 9 August 2022).

who claims to be sympathetic to the concept of a God who heals, yet he states:

> The success rates of contemporary healers, their interpretations of faith, the use of the name of Jesus and their emphasis on the significance of sin and Satan with regard to sickness find less harmony with the healing ministry of Jesus.[3]

Thirdly, these same facts represent failure in the view of many supporters of the continuance of supernatural healing, a group to which the author belongs, in that they appear to be contrary to the New Testament healing experiences of Jesus Christ and His followers. In an attempt to explain the lack of success in this ministry, it is the purpose of this work initially to examine the spectrum of Christian theology related to Christian healing. This examination will involve us addressing and answering certain pertinent questions. As Christians, we should not be surprised at the concept of necessary suffering. The Scriptures appear to teach that suffering is inevitable. But does suffering originate with or glorify God? Should enduring chronic sickness be considered an essential part of such suffering? And while God may use such sickness as a punishment for unbelievers[4] and the wilfully disobedient,[5] does He send it upon Christians, or should we consider it to be primarily from a diabolical source? What is the nature of the specific provision made through the past suffering of Jesus Christ whereby our sicknesses have been

---

3. Warrington, Keith, *Jesus the Healer: Paradigm or Unique Phenomenon?* (Carlisle: Paternoster, 2000), p.22.
4. Examples of whom are the Egyptians who oppressed and enslaved the Israelites.
5. 'However, if you do not obey the LORD your God and do not carefully follow his commands and decrees . . . the LORD will strike you with wasting disease, with fever and inflammation . . . The LORD will afflict you with the boils of Egypt and with tumours, festering sores and the itch, from which you cannot be cured' (Deuteronomy 28:15,22,27).

atoned for, and how is that provision appropriated? As a consequence of the way we answer this question, is there a tension between receiving divine healing by faith and relying on medical and surgical means? Is there a reason to expect that healing should occur in a miraculous and instantaneous fashion through a spoken word or a touch, in a similar manner to the healing accounts recorded in the New Testament? How does prayer for healing operate in accordance with James 5?

We shall then examine how this theology in turn dictates the practices of those churches and organisations that are engaged in the Christian healing ministry and how the healing ministry operates within local churches, dependent upon the beliefs found in those churches. These practices range from praying for doctors and nurses, and that medication will work, through praying and laying hands on the sick person, and anointing with oil, to rebuking the sickness and casting out spirits of infirmity. Having examined a broad range of beliefs and practices, and having concluded that it is generally God's will to heal and that the supernatural gifts, which include healing, are still in operation, we shall identify some hindrances to healing. What are those individual/personal, local church, community and global issues that limit the success of our healing ministries? For example, how does the attitude of a sick individual hinder or prevent a healing taking place? Does geographical location dictate the level of success or failure one might expect in the Christian healing ministry? Can a dearth of prayer in the Church at large be a contributing factor to the failure of a healing ministry? Is it usually God's will to bring healing or not? *Is there historic offence by the established Church towards the Person of the Holy Spirit that requires a large-scale renunciation and repentance*? Before we conclude, we shall look at the pastoral problem associated with an individual not being healed, despite the attempts, the faith, and often the pronouncements, of the faithful.

In making this journey, we shall look at personal testimonies of healing that illustrate the theological arguments being made. We shall refer in passing to topics relating to Christian healing which seem to be lacking in publications on the subject, such as:

- Was Jesus ever sick?
- Are there specific declarations that are unbiblical and, therefore, should not be made?
- Did Jesus pray for the sick or simply deal with the disease?
- Does God deal with injuries in a different way from sicknesses and diseases?

The Fact of Failure

Apart from those ministering in a small number of specific geographical areas, most honest practitioners in the field of Christian healing in our developed world would not claim a high success rate. The increased level of physical health experienced by individuals who have sought Christian healing through the churches that offer a healing ministry, relative to those using solely medical means, appears to be so small that it is too difficult to measure. If Christian healing were presently to take place with the quality and in the quantity achieved by Jesus and His first disciples, then our hospitals would not be so crowded, our waiting lists would not be so long and our medical practitioners would not be so overworked.[6] As it is, medical people, even those who are committed Christians, are reluctant to verify those cases that are claimed to be successful healings, preferring to use terms such as 'spontaneous remission', 'temporary alleviation' or 'positive response to treatment' to explain any improvement. These terms are all used in the concluding chapter, written by Professor Verna Wright, MD, FRCP, of Peter Masters' very sceptical book.[7] Alternatively, a 'psychosomatic illness' may be blamed for the condition in the first place. Furthermore, it is a fact that hundreds of Christians all over the world die every day as a result of diseases that would have been curable not only by Jesus during the time of His earthly ministry, but also by His apostles and their converts. Warrington states: 'The dissimilarity in success rates between believers then and today is significant and inexplicable if both groups received the same command.'[8]

For many people, the mark of authentic Christian healing is when all are healed, a mark which Warrington helpfully refutes.[9] However, Luke records Peter's summary of Jesus' ministry: 'God anointed Jesus of Nazareth with the Holy

---

6. This work is being edited during what seems to be the tail-end of a global pandemic, so these issues are very pertinent.
7. Masters, Peter, *The Healing Epidemic* (London: Wakeman, 1988).
8. Warrington, p.150.
9. See Warrington, p.161. Generally, the gospel writers tell us Jesus healed all who came or were brought to Him. However, there are implied non-healings, which we see, for example, in the account of Jesus encountering the lack of faith in His home town of Nazareth, where they were too familiar with His family background to accept Him as the Anointed One. When Jesus healed the woman with the haemorrhage, His disciples were mildly amused when He asked the question, 'Who touched Me?' Many had touched Him from every angle but only one had been healed, because only one had touched Him with healing faith. Also, only one was healed out of all the invalids who waited at the Pool of Bethesda for the waters to be troubled. On one occasion, Jesus appeared to be reluctant to heal the daughter of a Gentile. In studying the remainder of the New Testament, it appears to us that Trophemus was sick to the point of death before eventually recovering; Paul had a sickness, some believe an eye condition, that occasioned him to stay in Galatia until he recovered; and Timothy seemingly had stomach problems.

Ghost and with power: who went about doing good and healing *all that were oppressed* of the devil; for God was with him' (Acts 10:38 KJV, emphasis added). Matthew's gospel narrative seems to endorse this view in particularly strong terms. In Matthew 4:23, we read that Jesus healed *all* kinds of illness and disease and in the following verse we read He healed *all* who came to Him, some from as far away as Syria. In Matthew 8, after the record of the healing of Peter's mother-in-law, the evangelist tells how, on that evening, many demonised and sick people came to Jesus and He healed them *all*, and *all* the evil spirits fled. In Matthew 12:15, we read that Jesus healed *all* the sick from among those who had followed Him. Matthew 15:30 seems to imply that *all* the lame, blind, crippled, dumb and others that were brought to Jesus were healed. The 100 per cent success rate achieved by Jesus is recorded as having been carried on by His followers in Luke's Acts of the Apostles, where we read in 5:16, regarding the sick and the demonised brought to the apostles, that 'they were healed every one' (KJV); it is also evident in the ministry of Paul the apostle (Acts 28:9). Edward Gross is emphatic that we do not read in Scripture of any who came to Christ or the apostles for healing and did not[10] eventually[11] receive it. 'Jesus was not selective, but healed everyone presented to him. There is no instance of a sick person being brought to Jesus whom he did not heal.'[12] Gross

---

10. An interesting possible exception may be Simon the Leper whose home Jesus visited. Despite his obvious acquaintance with Jesus, there is no evidence that he was healed since he apparently had no sense of gratitude towards Jesus (unlike the sinful woman who wept at Jesus' feet in Simon's presence).
11. The gospel narratives tell us that, while Jesus was on the Mount of Transfiguration with Peter, James and John, the other disciples were unable to heal a boy brought to them by a desperate father. Upon His return, Jesus Himself dealt with the condition, but it is interesting to note that the apostles failed first time around! We will revisit this episode later.
12. Gross, Edward, N., *Miracles, Demons and Spiritual Warfare* (Grand Rapids, MI: Baker, 1990), p.62.

nevertheless acknowledges failure by the disciples after Jesus' Transfiguration,[13] an incident that we will examine at a later stage. One writer puts the need for total success in the healing ministry in the strongest possible terms:

> I am certain that the person who claims to have a gift of healing discredits the person of Christ, if (and it is a big 'if') there were ninety-nine successes and only one failure, even that would discredit Christ because He *never* fails. If we say to a man, 'In the name of Jesus rise up and walk,' and he continues to lie at the Beautiful Gate of the Temple, that is a failure that reflects upon the person and the power of Christ,[14] and this is happening all the time.[15]

William Nolen, a medical doctor who made a prolonged investigation into the healing ministry of the late Kathryn Kuhlman, interprets and records the personal anguish associated with the failure to heal:

> As I stood in the corridor watching the hopeless cases leave, seeing the tears in the eyes of the parents as they pushed their crippled children to

---

13. Gross, p.62. He explains this recorded failure by the disciples, together with other assumed failures, as part of their learning process. Although he states, 'These believers learned their lessons well,' he does not allow for contemporary believers to undergo such learning. He says, 'After Pentecost there is no instance of a person with the gift of healing ever failing when attempting to heal another person' (see p.66). He could have claimed, 'After the Resurrection there is no instance of a person with the gift of healing ever failing when attempting to heal another person', but presumably he would have had to defend the idea that there is healing in the Atonement, an issue we shall deal with in a later section of this work.
14. On one occasion in the New Testament, we read of the name of Jesus being used unsuccessfully during an attempted exorcism by the seven sons of Sceva. On that occasion, neither the person nor the power of Christ was discredited, but rather the would-be 'healers' were disgraced and the name of Jesus was greatly honoured in the region as a consequence. See Acts 19:13-20.
15. Professor Verna Wright, 'A Medical View of Miraculous Healing', in Masters, p.217. Presumably the professor does not speak for an individual who has received a 100 per cent cure!

the elevators, I wished Miss Kuhlman had been with me . . . I wondered if she sincerely felt that the joy of those 'cured' of bursitis and arthritis compensated for the anguish of those left with their withered legs, their imbecilic children, their cancers of the liver.[16]

In Singapore, the Anglican Church experienced a wave of healing in the early 1970s, when many who had been suffering from chronic crippling conditions for several years began to walk unaided. The movement was not without its critics, and John Woolmer, himself an Anglican and an advocate of Christian healing, states:

The controversy however centred around the 'healings'. It is true that in proportion to those who came for healing, the number who claimed to be healed was not very high . . . Among the perplexing questions asked were 'Can these claims of healing be substantiated, or are they illusions or even frauds?' 'Were they of God even if they were done in the Name of Jesus?' 'What about those who were not healed?'[17]

One possible reason given for failure is that not all those gifted with healing can heal every type of condition. The late Francis MacNutt,[18] for example, claimed to have

---

16. Nolen, William, *Healing: A Doctor in Search of a Miracle* (New York, NY: Random House, 1974), p.60.
17. Woolmer, John, *Healing and Deliverance* (London: Monarch, 1999), p.205. Note how, despite the fact that some were unquestionably healed in the name of Jesus, the critics still questioned whether these healings were of God. Presumably they were thinking of Jesus' own warning of how, on the last day, some who have never known Him will claim to have cast out demons and have done miracles in His name but will be regarded by Him as 'workers of iniquity'.
18. Francis Scott MacNutt (1925–2020) was an American former Roman Catholic priest. Associated with the Catholic Charismatic Renewal, he was an author of books on healing prayer, including *Healing*, *The Healing Reawakening* and *Deliverance From Evil Spirits*.

greater success when ministering to people with bone conditions and those with chest and abdominal complaints, while the late C. Peter Wagner[19] claimed to have a speciality for healing those with pelvic and spinal abnormalities.[20] This reasoning when applied to non-healing, although consistent with Paul's reference to 'gifts [plural] of healing' in 1 Corinthians 12, is viewed sceptically by many Evangelical scholars. Similar scepticism applies when a specific condition is not completely healed in an individual. Gross comments:

> We are certain that any gift which manifests the supernatural power of God will not fail. Failure to accomplish our own will arises from either a lack of power or a lack of wisdom, but the omnipotent Spirit of God has no such deficiency. The gift of healing is confirmed, then, by the ability to *completely* heal a person in the name of Jesus.[21]

An improvement in a condition as a result of the administering of Christian healing (particularly by those who claim to have a gift of healing), despite the obvious relief on the part of the sufferer, is therefore not considered by critics such as Gross, Nolen, Masters, et al. as being the authentic outworking of the New Testament spiritual gift of healing.

The author has seen God's healing in operation and has received personal healing in a miraculous way, which is recorded later in this work, together with other testimonies

---

19. Charles Peter Wagner (15 August 1930 – 21 October 2016) was a theologian, missiologist, missionary, writer, teacher and church-growth specialist best known for his controversial writings on spiritual warfare.
20. Wagner, C. Peter, *Warfare Prayer* (Tunbridge Wells: Monarch, 1992), see p.215.
21. Gross, p.60.

of healing. He has also been personally involved over an extended period of time in ministering Christian healing individually, but not exclusively, to numerous seriously ill cancer patients. The majority of these individuals, men, women and children, exhibited exemplary faith in the One who heals, and the author and the other Christians who ministered at various times had expectant faith for their healing. Yet most of these sick individuals have since died, several are fighting the disease with the daily help of specialist cancer drugs and a small proportion have made, or are on the road to making, a complete recovery, many having also undergone a programme of surgery and/or chemotherapy and/or radiotherapy.

Most biblical scholars would not regard this level of success as being comparable to the healing ministry of the New Testament. However, how we assess failure, together with how we administer healing (if at all), will be substantially driven by our theology. This will take into account our Christian belief with regard to the nature of God, His will and the gifting of the Church in the area of healing. If, for example, the ministry of Christ and His apostles was a unique ministry associated with a unique event and period in history, then it is not surprising that those claiming to practise the same miraculous gifts after the event and period have passed, are not seeing the expected results. This 'unique ministry' viewpoint is the basis of Warrington's previously cited work *Jesus the Healer* where he draws the conclusion:

> Rather than assuming a direct line between Jesus' practice and contemporary healing, the uniqueness of his ministry is to be recognized and affirmed.

> Rather than viewing Jesus as a healing archetype, the evidence dictates that his healing ministry was unique.[22]

A similar lack of positive results will apply if the gospel miracles are regarded merely as being a guide for Christians to care for those in less fortunate circumstances than themselves, which is Martyn Percy's suggestion:

> The Gospel miracles are to be understood as 'a record of Christ reaching out to the marginalized, dispossessed, cast out and cursed in society and from faith communities'.[23]

Some conclude that God chooses only to work miraculously when medical and surgical expertise are not available,[24] in circumstances supposedly similar to those prevailing at the time of Jesus and the apostles, when many cures had not been discovered. Similar circumstances exist in the present-day, particularly with the scourge of HIV/AIDS. Christian communities in Africa, India, the Far East and South America have reported many miraculous cures in recent years, bolstering this argument. The recent, global Covid-19 pandemic which has suddenly regressed us to a point of need similar to that of New Testament times, as our hospitals struggled to cope while we attempted to roll out vaccination programmes. Irrespective of the present

---

22. Warrington, p.162.
23. Martyn Percy, cited in Warrington, p.4. This is basically a liberation theology approach, which, when taken to its ultimate conclusion, also reinterprets personal salvation as political liberation (see 'Liberation Theology' in Lane, A.N.S., *The Lion Concise Book* of *Christian Thought* [Tring: Lion, 1984], pp.249-251, where Lane refers to the work of Gustavo Gutiérrez and others).
24. Others believe that the option of divine healing should be considered only when medical and surgical means have been exhausted, citing the example of the woman recorded in Luke 8: 'And a woman was there who had been subject to bleeding for twelve years, but no one could heal her' (v.43). However, taken to its logical conclusion, this notion would suggest we should pray only when we have made every human effort to solve the issue that is concerning us – clearly unbiblical!

crisis, we can immediately dispense with this 'medical science replacement' baseline notion as being a reason for a lack of success in the area of miraculous healing. After all, the need for such healing is presently no less in our own Western communities. Here, new strains of disease seem to emerge as soon as each new cure is developed; and here, such conditions as depression,[25] stress-related ailments and post-viral conditions are on the increase at an alarming rate, pointing to a need not only for healing in the traditional sense but also for inner healing.[26] This fact has brought about an increased focus on the seeming requirement for, and practice of, a wide spectrum of healing skills within Christian healing ministry, working in conjunction with prayer and the gifts of healing.

If, as Christians, we are called to suffer with Christ, and if sickness and disease form a valid constituent part of that suffering,[27] then in offering healing[28] we may be working against the purposes of God for our lives. In seeking healing, we may be attempting to deny Him His right to refine us, as His sons and daughters, through trials and various modes of suffering, including sickness and disease.

---

25. This is the clinical form of depression, not simply feeling low. We feel low when we lose jobs, we have strained relationships, our sports team loses(!) and so on. Under the circumstances, this is a normal emotion in the same way that happiness is the natural response when things are going well: a work promotion, the birth of a child, our team wins; no one would think that was unnatural. However, when things are good and we still feel down, that indicates the illness of depression. It is why expressions such as 'Look on the bright side' and 'Pull yourself together' are not helpful to the sufferer. It is true that this kind of illness is on the increase, but let us not make the mistake of thinking that depression is a 21st-century ailment; the psalmist laments, 'Why, my soul, are you downcast? Why so disturbed within me?' (Psalm 43:5). The antithesis and antidote to this kind of depression is the 'joy of the Lord', which is a deep joy that is felt even in the face of persecution and death. It was this human state that enabled Paul and Silas to sing hymns of praise to God in the inner precincts of a prison in Philippi (Acts 16).
26. In severe cases, it is recognised that the root causes of certain illnesses have to be dealt with through the counselling work of psychologists or psychiatrists, and through a whole range of alternative means of treatment. *Question: how would Jesus have handled these ailments?*
27. A concept that is argued against in the following chapter.
28. Or, indeed, doing anything other than actively discouraging sick and infirm persons from seeking surgical or medical advice or pain relief.

21

If, on the other hand, we believe that sickness and disease are primarily the result of sin – original, universal and individual – as is the conclusion of the following section, and are major offensive weapons originated, orchestrated and utilised by the devil against a humanity that is made in the image of its Creator, and that if Christ was revealed to destroy all the works of the devil, then it follows that the power of sickness has been destroyed and that healing can be received through faith. If, through the cross, Jesus Christ provided not only for our spiritual health but also for our physical health because 'by his wounds we are healed',[29] then this healing should be pursued personally with vigour and encouraged for others, using such means as are both practical and biblical. If we have been commissioned through Mark 16:15-18 to lay our 'hands on the sick, [so that] they shall recover' (KJV) through the empowering of a 'purpose-built' spiritual gift, then we are living in disobedience if we are not practising a New Testament healing ministry in our churches. As a result, many could be suffering unnecessarily, having been led to believe that their sicknesses are ultimately from God.[30]

---

29. Isaiah 53:5b.
30. There is a much debated passage in 1 Corinthians 11:27ff where Paul is telling the church at Corinth why some of their members have grown sick and some have died. Traditionally, this has been explained as the judgement of God upon believers who have not eaten the Lord's Supper in a worthy manner, 'not discerning the body and blood of the Lord Jesus'. This view is supported by the account in Acts where we read that death came upon Ananias and Sapphira as a judgement for lying to the Holy Spirit. However, Jesus' dying breath was a petition to His Father for forgiveness for those who humiliated Him and destroyed His physical body. Six weeks later, the Father answered that prayer when Peter publicly confronted many of those very same offenders, they were 'cut to the heart' and subsequently repented, believed and were saved. It is mysterious, then, that such a serious judgement could have been dealt out to those who had somehow dishonoured His *sacramental* body. The most plausible explanation of this difficult passage that is consistent with our understanding of the nature of God's forgiveness (although debatably not the best exegesis of the passage) is offered by McCrossan, a classical Pentecostal who vigorously argues that healing is in the Atonement. He explains that many in that church had become ill and some had died because they failed to discern (in that, in Christ's broken body in addition to His blood shed for the remission of sin, which the sacrament of the Lord's Supper celebrates), there was healing made available for them. See McCrossan, T.J. (re-edited Hicks, R. and Hagin, K.), *Bodily Healing and the Atonement* (New York, NY: Faith Library, 1982).

There are obvious, mutually exclusive aspects to this summary of belief systems, and the content of our healing practices, together with our assessments of the successes and failures experienced, will be fuelled by those beliefs. It is of paramount importance, therefore, to examine the constituent elements and biblical bases for each opposing theological view and the range of beliefs in between, together with the corresponding Christian healing practices.

Christian Beliefs With Regard to Sickness and Healing

Sickness and Its Purpose in Suffering

Firstly, it is of prime importance to examine the Christian's undisputed call to a life that will include suffering as inevitable. This is because Christ Himself suffered and calls the members of His Church to be followers in His path. There is a general theology of suffering evident in both Old and New Testaments. Scripture abounds with passages about the purposes of suffering. With regard to the unbeliever and the disobedient, Scripture teaches that often God sends pain and affliction as a means of judgement for sin:

> Consider now: who, being innocent, has ever perished? Where were the upright ever destroyed? As I have observed, those who plough evil and those who sow trouble reap it. At the breath of God they perish; at the blast of his anger they are no more. (Job 4:7-9)

Sometimes such pain and affliction may succeed in turning the individual back to God (e.g. Jonah), or in bringing a person or a nation to salvation (see Zechariah 12). In terms of helping us to understand why the righteous suffer, the Scriptures also have something to say. Sometimes

God will allow the righteous to be afflicted as a means of chastisement:

> Blessed is the one you discipline, LORD, the one you teach from your law; you grant them relief from days of trouble, till a pit is dug for the wicked. For the LORD will not reject his people; he will never forsake his inheritance. (Psalm 94:12-14)

A similar sentiment is found in the New Testament. The writer states:

> My son, do not make light of the Lord's discipline, and do not lose heart when he rebukes you, because the Lord disciplines the one he loves, and he chastens everyone he accepts as his son. (Hebrews 12:5-6)

On some occasions, the purpose of human affliction is to demonstrate to Satan that there are those who serve God because they love Him, and not because it pays to do so. This was evident in the case of Job:

> One day the angels came to present themselves before the LORD, and Satan also came with them. The LORD said to Satan, 'Where have you come from?' Satan answered the LORD, 'From roaming through the earth, and going to and fro on it.' Then the LORD said to Satan, 'Have you considered my servant Job? There is no one on earth like him; he is blameless and upright, a man who fears God and shuns evil.' 'Does Job fear God for nothing?' Satan replied. 'Have you not put a hedge around him and his household and everything he has? You have blessed the work of his hands, so that his flocks and herds are spread

throughout the land. But now stretch out your hand and strike everything he has, and he will surely curse you to your face.' (Job 1:6-11)

According to the apostle Peter, suffering promotes sanctification:

Therefore, since Christ suffered in his body, arm yourselves also with the same attitude, because whoever suffers in the body has finished with sin. As a result, they do not live the rest of their earthly lives for evil human desires, but rather for the will of God. (1 Peter 4:1-2)

It does so in various ways, such as refining the Christian's faith:

In all this you greatly rejoice, though now for a little while you may have had to suffer grief in all kinds of trials. These have come so that the proven genuineness of your faith – of greater worth than gold, which perishes even though refined by fire – may result in praise, glory and honour when Jesus Christ is revealed. (1 Peter 1:6-7)

Suffering promotes Christian development in such attributes as endurance and perseverance:

Consider it pure joy, my brothers, whenever you face trials of many kinds, because you know that the testing of your faith produces perseverance. Let perseverance finish its work so that you may be mature and complete, not lacking anything. (James 1:2-4)

And we boast in the hope of the glory of God. Not only so, but we also glory in our sufferings, because we know that suffering produces perseverance; perseverance, character; and character, hope. (Romans 5:2-4)

Suffering is instrumental in helping God's people to understand His sovereign character more fully:

Then Job replied to the LORD: 'I know that you can do all things; no purpose of yours can be thwarted. You asked, "Who is this that obscures my plans without knowledge?" Surely I spoke of things I did not understand, things too wonderful for me to know. You said, "Listen now, and I will speak; I will question you, and you shall answer me." My ears had heard of you but now my eyes have seen you. Therefore I despise myself and repent in dust and ashes.' (Job 42:1-6)

It also gives the Christian an opportunity to imitate Christ:

It is better, if it is God's will, to suffer for doing good than for doing evil. For Christ also suffered once for sins, the righteous for the unrighteous, to bring you to God. (1 Peter 3:17-18)

If any of these examples of suffering occurs in the life of the Christian in an obvious way, it will be evidence of sanctification, because sanctification is developed through affliction. On some occasions, God's purposes in afflicting His followers is to prepare them for the judgement of their works in the context of future rewards. Believers will someday give an account of their works before the Lord, and affliction is seen as a means to help them prepare, such that, on that day, their faith will be found to honour and glorify Jesus at His coming, as previously referenced in 1

Peter 1:6-7. If that happens, the Christian will be rewarded, so affliction ultimately is a means to reward in such cases.

Finally, God uses affliction as a prelude to the exaltation of the Christian. The theme of suffering giving way to glory is prevalent throughout Scripture, especially in 1 Peter. The example of Christ is of course the pattern exhorted by the earlier quotation from 1 Peter 3 (see also verses 19-22) and Paul's classic 'Servant' passage:

> Not looking to your own interests but each of you to the interests of the others. In your relationships with one another, have the same mindset as Christ Jesus: who, being in very nature God, did not consider equality with God something to be used to his own advantage;[31] rather, he made himself nothing by taking the very nature of a servant, being made in human likeness. And being found in appearance as a man, he humbled himself by becoming obedient to death – even death on a cross! Therefore God exalted him to the highest place and gave him the name that is above every name, that at the name of Jesus every knee should bow, in heaven and on earth and under the earth, and every tongue acknowledge that Jesus Christ is Lord, to the glory of God the Father. (Philippians 2:4-11)

---

31. Note the aspiration of the 'second Adam' relative to the first Adam who desired to exalt himself and become as a god, and as a result was humiliated and brought humiliation on the whole human race. Whereas Jesus 'made himself of no reputation' (KJV) and underwent humiliation, and was, as a result, exalted to the highest place. Larry Huch (an American non-denominational pastor, televangelist, and who is the founder and senior pastor of DFW New Beginnings in Bedford, Texas, along with his wife Tiz) sums it up by commenting (on the God Channel) that, in the garden (of Gethsemane), Jesus said, 'Not my will but Yours be done,' whereas Adam, in the garden (of Eden), said, 'Not Your will but mine be done.'

God desires to exalt the Christian who is humble before Him, even if that humbling involves affliction: 'Humble yourselves, therefore, under God's mighty hand, that he may lift you up in due time' (1 Peter 5:6). There is also a significant body of teaching with regard to suffering that is obvious in the writings of Paul and that is consistent with this general theology of suffering. Luke's account of the life of Paul, as recorded in the book of Acts, catalogues much of Paul's personal suffering. His words of encouragement to his converts in Syrian Antioch included, 'We must go through many hardships to enter the kingdom of God' (Acts 14:22). Correspondingly, Paul certainly does not gloss over the cold fact of Christian suffering in his writings. Indeed, it can be argued from Paul that suffering is an essential element of the Christian experience. In Romans 8:16-17, he writes, 'The Spirit himself testifies with our spirit that we are God's children. Now if we are children, then we are heirs – heirs of God and co-heirs with Christ, if indeed we share in his sufferings in order that we may also share in his glory.' This passage seems to indicate that our level of glorification in the future state is in direct proportion to the duration or intensity of our present transient suffering. In this particular aspect of Paul's theology of suffering, the previously cited example of Christ is the pattern (Philippians 2:5-11). His suffering and humiliation as the One who emptied Himself and became obedient to death on a cross led to Him being exalted to the highest place and for Him to have been given the name that is above every name, culminating in the eventual, future universal acknowledgement that 'He is Lord'. Another aspect of this theology of suffering is expressed in Philippians 1:29, where Paul writes: 'For it has been granted to you on behalf of Christ not only to believe in him, but also to suffer for him,' thus linking personal suffering with personal belief. In Philippians 3:8, Paul contrasts the insignificance of suffering the loss of all things with the significance of gaining Christ. The inevitability of suffering is further emphasised in Paul's analogy of the Church as a human body in 1 Corinthians 12, where he states in v.26, 'If one part suffers, every part suffers with it', indicating that even when we are not suffering personally, there is a sense in which we are participating in the suffering of others. This idea is illustrated in a practical way in Paul's later writings to the same church, when he says, 'And our hope for you is firm, because we know that just as you share in our sufferings, so also you share in our comfort' (2 Corinthians 1:7). He goes on to refer to a specific example which has been lost to us, but of which the original recipients of his letter appear to know some of the details. In verse 8, he states: 'For we do not want you to be unaware . . . of our affliction . . . in Asia, that we were burdened excessively . . . so that we despaired even of life' (NASB 1995).[32] There is a further dimension to Paul's theology evident earlier in this chapter, in that the experience of affliction and pain offer an empathetic opportunity for the Christian to minister to others who are undergoing affliction (vv.3-4) and comfort others while specifically availing them of the means by which we ourselves have been comforted. The Greek word *paracleses* translated 'comfort' has the double meaning of

---

32. At first sight, it is natural to assume that Paul is referring to the uproar at Ephesus (Acts 19); however, there is no scriptural evidence that Paul was in any acute personal danger (see Tasker, R.V.G., *2 Corinthians*, Tyndale New Testament Commentaries [Leicester: IVP, 1983], p.42). Charles Caldwell Ryrie suggests some serious, possibly contagious, illness because Paul and his companions despaired of their lives (*The Ryrie Study Bible: NASB* [Chicago, IL: Moody, 1976], p. 1753). However, there is no evidence of this either, other than the fact that, at one point, one of Paul's companions was left behind because of his ill health (2 Timothy 4:20) and one almost died (Philippians 2:25-30).

encouragement and *consolation*.[33] This aspect of Christian suffering further relates to our following in the footsteps of Christ who was 'A man of suffering, and familiar with pain' (Isaiah 53:3) and one who, in His intercessory role, continues to be 'Touched with the feeling of our infirmities' (Hebrews 4:15 KJV).

As an illustration, it is worthwhile recounting, from the author's previously written journal, an event from Cali, Colombia, experienced during his first visit there in 2004:

> The one thing I was aware of was how many people had committed to pray for us. The need for such prayer was made abundantly clear to me on the fourth morning of our trip. We were being housed in the homes of local church members, and I was sharing accommodation with Malcolm Hamilton, a brother from Plymouth, England. We were staying with Elirio and his wife Esperanta in what had once been a nice neighbourhood but that had subsequently become run down. The team that I was part of had been to pray and sing praise over Cali at one of the nearby mountain peaks, where a statue of Christ overlooks the city; a replica of Christ the King in Rio de Janeiro. Our team leader, Paul Bennison, had had a phone call from a prayer partner in the US. She had had a vision of the team walking through a minefield. Shortly afterwards another call led our leader to make the announcement that Malcolm and myself could not go back to Elirio's home. He informed the team: 'Shortly after Paul and Malcolm left this

---

33. Tasker, p.41.

morning four armed men came looking for them.' At first it was not clear if this was because we were Christians, but as it transpired, it was our money and/or passports that they were after. Paul told us that if they had been particularly nasty, they might have abducted us for a ransom. I learned after returning home from that visit that during that period, out of all the kidnappings that occurred in the world, 45 per cent took place in Colombia.

Elirio had been in the house on his own and had been tied up and shoved under his bed by the intruders. His house had been trashed and Elirio's savings and wristwatch had been taken. His response to the gunmen had been: 'You can't steal from these men – they are God's missionaries to our city.' As it transpired, the only item of ours that was stolen was my mobile phone. It had refused to charge the previous day – a problem that had been becoming worse for some time – so I had left it behind, reckoning it had finally given up the ghost. Needless to say, O2, my UK service provider, replaced it free of charge on my return to the UK. A scripture we had been given (by someone to whom the incident was unknown) was Psalm 124: 'If the LORD had not been on our side when people attacked us, they would have swallowed us alive ... We have escaped like a bird from the fowler's snare.' Two local churchmen retrieved our belongings and we were moved to a 'safe house'. I felt guilty, however, about the fact that we had been the source of Elirio's experience of hardship. We were not encouraged to return to his neighbourhood and so we had been unable to speak with him after the event. However, several days later he appeared at one of the meetings we were taking part in. He was elated! He punched the air as he recalled his experience of the four gunmen: 'I rejoice, God is my Father, He has given us the victory!' he shouted. He was convinced that his experience of suffering at the hands of these men was proof of his divine son-ship. 'Endure hardship as discipline; God is treating you as his children. For what children are not disciplined by their father?' (Hebrews 12:7).

Paul the apostle describes the nature of Christian ministry in 2 Corinthians 4 and in doing so he includes the fact that we are 'afflicted in every way, but not crushed; perplexed, but not despairing; persecuted, but not forsaken; struck down, but not destroyed' (vv.8-9 NASB 1995). In chapter 6 of the same letter, Paul associates suffering with servanthood: 'As servants of God, in much endurance, in afflictions, in hardships, in distresses, in beatings, in imprisonments, in tumults, in labours, in sleeplessness, in hunger . . .' (vv.4-5 NASB 1995). In the same context of servanthood, Paul elaborates further upon the nature and sources of these sufferings:

> I have worked much harder, been in prison more frequently, been flogged more severely, and been exposed to death again and again. Five times I received from the Jews the forty lashes minus one. Three times I was beaten with rods, once I was pelted with stones, three times I was shipwrecked, I spent a night and a day in the open sea, I have

been constantly on the move. I have been in danger from rivers, in danger from bandits, in danger from my fellow Jews, in danger from Gentiles; in danger in the city, in danger in the country, in danger at sea; and in danger from false believers. I have laboured and toiled and have often gone without sleep; I have known hunger and thirst and have often gone without food; I have been cold and naked. Besides everything else, I face daily the pressure of my concern for all the churches. (2 Corinthians 11:23-28)

Some commentators regard these verses as a contextual preface to Paul sharing with his readers about his 'thorn in the flesh' (12:7 KJV). Thus, there is a scholarly view with regard to Paul's 'thorn' which concludes that sickness in the life of the Christian is often used by God as a means of sanctification, a view that the author will later dispute.[34] If we, as part of our Christian healing ministry, seek to eradicate a sanctification; sickness sent by God, such a healing ministry will be marked with the levels of 'success' that we are actually seeing presently because in a majority of cases we will be opposing God's will. *So, this theology of 'non-healing', which links the suffering caused by sickness in a positive way to Christian sanctification,*

---

34. Madden, Peter J., *The Wigglesworth Standard: The Standard for God's End-time Army* (Springdale, PA: Whitaker House, 1993). Used with permission. All rights reserved. www.whitakerhouse.com. Madden quotes Smith Wigglesworth: 'I visited a woman who had been suffering for many years. She was all twisted up with rheumatism and had been in bed two years. I asked her, "What makes you lie here?" She said, "I've come to the conclusion that I have a thorn in the flesh." I said, "To what wonderful degree of righteousness have you attained that you must have a thorn in the flesh? Have you had such an abundance of divine revelations that there is a danger of your being exalted above measure?" [See 2 Corinthians 12:7-99.]. She said, "I believe it is the Lord who is causing me to suffer." I said, "You believe it is the Lord's will for you to suffer, but you are trying to get out of it as quickly as you can. You have medicine bottles all over the place. Disease is not caused by righteousness, but by sin"' (p.179).

may be the biblical explanation for an apparent lack of successful healing ministries! In other words, it is because the sovereignty of God is opposing such 'success'. How sound is this premise? It is reputed that holiness preachers A.J. Gordon and A.B. Simpson, who were the pioneers of early Pentecostalism and who advocated the availability of divine healing for all Christians, became ill and died as a result. This occurred despite them personally claiming their healing and having hands laid on them by their contemporaries who were gifted in the area of healing:

> Both were overcome by sickness and died in spite of many contrary prayers. Both fell under a spiritual cloud in sickness, concluding personal sin. How much better to be resigned to the will of God and relax happily in the will of God.[35]

However, in truth, very few Christians 'relax happily in the will of God' if they are sick, whether they believe in the prospect of Christian healing or not. Few refuse painkillers, medicines, antibiotics or even surgery and life-saving treatments where these 'means' promise a cure or a relief from pain. Jesus, however, our life example, refused to have His crucifixion pains dulled by wine mixed with gall: 'There [at Golgotha] they offered Jesus wine to drink, mixed with gall; but after tasting it, he refused to drink it' (Matthew 27:34). To be consistent, these previously mentioned means of alleviation and pain relief should also be refused if there is the possibility that the illness is a chastisement from God or a means of sanctification. Many Christians, as is alleged was the case with Gordon

---

35. Douglas, Alban, *God's Answers to Man's Questions* (Greenville, SC: W.D. Kennedy, 1981), p.202.

and Simpson, 'fall under a spiritual cloud during a time of sickness, concluding that it is the result of personal sin', not because they have not been miraculously healed, but because they have become sick in the first place. There is also, perhaps, a Christian view that there is little sanctification apparent in many degenerative illnesses, for example, in an affliction such as the dementia caused by Alzheimer's disease. Humour the author for a moment and picture the scene in Jerusalem as Jesus of Nazareth visits the Pool of Bethesda, where He meets a man who has been an invalid for thirty-eight years. When Jesus sees him lying there and learns that he has been in this condition for a long time, He asks him, 'Do you want to get well?' 'No, Sir,' the invalid replies. 'I have been given this disease to glorify God and I am determined to suffer on!' (See John 11:4.) *The thought of this is ridiculous!*

In a work entitled *The Thorn in the Flesh*, R.T. Kendall looks at contemporary problems that he describes as 'thorns'. He cites loneliness, unhappy employment, an enemy, a handicap or disability, unhappy living conditions, a sexual misgiving, an unhappy marriage, *a chronic illness*, personality problems, money matters and an unwanted calling. Obviously, based on this listing, Kendall regards sickness as being a valid constituent of Christian suffering. Romans chapter 8 has been cited above with reference to the inevitability of Christian suffering. However, in verses 35-39 of the same chapter, Paul assures the Christian of the love of Christ in the midst of suffering and, in doing so, cites 'tribulation, or distress, or persecution, or famine, or nakedness, or peril, or sword' (KJV) as potential suffering. He does not, however, include sickness in his listing. It is significant that sickness is omitted from every other list of sufferings compiled by Paul. Furthermore, those sufferings listed are all examples of transient suffering that were, in Paul's case, interspersed with seasons of great joy amidst persecution. This is not true of the nature of chronic illnesses that some Christians believe they are called to bear, like the persistent illness that Paul's 'thorn in the flesh' is considered by some scholars to be.[36] Lenski, on the other hand, supports the belief that Paul was not frequently ill. He observes:

> A sick man is never impressive and assuring. A sick man who claims miraculous powers and heals others, while he himself remains sick, would certainly raise serious doubts regarding any message he might bring.[37]

In support of this belief, Tasker states:

> It must be acknowledged that the general impression of Paul that the reader gains from his epistles, not least from 2 Corinthians, and from Acts, is of a man with an exceptionally strong constitution and remarkable powers of physical endurance. This is not really compatible with the view that he was the constant victim of a severe physical ailment.[38]

---

36. It is certainly true that Paul had suffered illness at one point, as he records in Galatians 4. It seems that he originally preached to the Galatians because he had an illness (a 'bodily illness', NASB). There is much scholarly speculation in relation to this passage, particularly in its alleged connection to the subject of Paul's 'thorn'. R. Alan Cole suggests that one possible translation of 'bodily illness' is 'bodily weakness' (*Galatians*, Tyndale New Testament Commentaries [Leicester: IVP, 1984], p.56). If the visit to Galatia occurred shortly after Paul's stoning (which is recorded in Acts 14), then the weakness may have been due to this. As Paul recuperated among the Galatians, preaching and teaching, gradually growing stronger, his deliverance from death would have been regarded as being correspondingly miraculous. Yet this set of circumstances, whatever it entailed, was not described by Paul as a trial to him, but rather *as a trial to the Galatians!*
37. R.C.H. Lenski, quoted in Vos, Howard F., *Galatians: A Call to Christian Liberty* (Columbus, OH: Lutheran Book Concern, 1937), p.78.
38. Tasker, p.175.

Despite the fact that Paul appears to have left Trophimus in Malta because of his illness (2 Timothy 4:20) and he records how Epaphroditus almost died due to severe illness (Philippians 2:25-30), he nevertheless believed in and operated in the gift of divine healing, demonstrating that the suffering attributed to sickness could be permanently alleviated for the Christian. This fact is often seen in the narrative of Luke's biographical account.

We must also acknowledge the fact that, from time to time, Christians just get sick because we are living in a fallen world. We should be encouraged to seek God's healing touch. The author has previously referred to the Covid-19 pandemic that has been indiscriminate in its rampage and has severely afflicted some of his close friends. One local pastor's story was captured by the local press:

> A North Belfast pastor who fought Covid-19 and won has said that God sent him a cleaner in hospital to help him pull through. Pastor Lee McClelland from The Ark Church said the domestic came to him and prayed for him when no one else could visit in isolation . . . He said: 'I was under incredible pressure, got drips up and all that they needed to do, but I remember those nights particularly, really crying out to the Lord and asked Him to help me and asked Him to even supernaturally just do something that would encourage me and bring me through. I remember the next day I had a night from hell and you've got to understand this in the isolation ward, when no one else can get in, when no one else, no pastor, no friend, no family members, when no one else was allowed in, God sent a cleaner.

He left that day and then he says this as he stood at the door. He says: 'Son, could I pray for you?' I says: 'Absolutely.' And as he began to pray at the door, he couldn't touch me, he began to ask God the Holy Ghost to visit me. He began to ask God to heal my body and touch my lungs. He stood at that doorway and he pleaded that God Almighty would spare my life and to continue to use me. And what was incredible was that, after he left, he periodically would walk past my window and give me a thumbs-up.

That night I remember I started to turn around. Could it have been the prayer of a cleaner?

Pastor McClelland said that as he began to feel better his appetite returned and he prayed to God for crisps and cola – and his prayers were answered.

He said: 'That night I began to desire a packet of prawn cocktail crisps, Tayto,[39] and I asked the Lord because no one could get to me. The next morning the cleaner came, he brought in a bag and in that bag was two oranges, a tin of Coke and a packet of prawn cocktail crisps!'[40]

The reader is encouraged to examine the scriptures that have been quoted in this section in their context and to conclude that there is no obvious scriptural connection between the suffering caused by sickness and the suffering

---

39. Tayto is a Northern Ireland brand of potato crisps (potato chips for those in the US) – highly recommended!
40. David O'Dornan, 'Pastor Lee McClelland credits his Covid-19 survival to cleaner's prayer', *Sunday Life,* 12 April 2020.

we are called to experience as Christians for the purpose of our sanctification through character building. If this is so, it is prudent to reject the premise that prolonged and chronic sicknesses are literally 'a necessary evil' in the life of the Christian, and for us to examine further the origin and nature of sickness to discover why it should be categorised differently from other forms of human suffering.

The Source of Sickness and Disease

What is the source of sickness? In the first two chapters of Genesis, we find a description of a world created by God, which He consistently describes as 'all very good'. We cannot contemplate that sickness existed in such a world; however, just as the advent of sin brought death, it also appears to have brought with it a myriad of degenerative measures, or curses, including sickness. We can generalise and collectively call these degenerative measures 'evil'. This notion of evil differs from the concept of evil as moral choice. We note that in Isaiah 45, God, through the prophet, declares, 'I have made the earth, and created man upon it: I, even my hands, have stretched out the heavens, and all their host I have commanded' (v.12 KJV). In this context, that is, of original creation, the prophecy also says: 'I . . . create darkness . . . I . . . create evil' (v.7 KJV). This statement represents God taking the 'responsibility for the presence of evil in the midst of His creation',[41] for the *possibility, but not the inevitability,* of evil as a moral choice (i.e. 'sin'). The tree of the knowledge of good and evil was there, present in the garden, when all was still 'very good'.

---

41. Fitch, William, *God & Evil: Studies in the Mystery of Suffering and Pain* (London: Pickering and Inglis, 1967), p.16.

> This is the first mention of 'evil' in the Bible [the tree of the knowledge of good and evil]. It is not yet an actuality in man's history. It is here only in a potential sense. Ten times already we have read the word 'good' ... Now we meet with something else – 'the tree of the knowledge of good and evil.' It grows at the heart of all this good creation.[42]

This, however, does not mean that God is the author of sin on the basis that sin is correctly defined as the making of a moral choice to engage in evil. Nor does He tempt His creation to make that choice, for 'God cannot be tempted by evil, nor does he tempt anyone' (James 1:13). One must look therefore for another entity, one that is the active agent of evil and the tempter of humankind into making a choice to embrace that evil. The evangelists purposefully record Jesus' temptation in the wilderness and identify Satan as the tempter. Jesus himself refers to Satan, or the devil, as the 'evil one' (Matthew 13:38) and describes the devil's character in greater detail in John 8:44. If he is the primary agent of evil, then it is entirely possible and consistent with his nature that he should be the originator and administrator of sickness and disease.

It is necessary, therefore, to confirm if, and then how, Satan administers sicknesses and diseases. The book of Job is an obvious starting point. However, we are not told in that book precisely how the afflictions of Job took place, other than that Satan was directly responsible. If we are to rely on the gospels, it is logical (but strangely not obvious to many Christians) to assume that the affliction of human beings with sickness and disease is accomplished

---

42. Fitch, p.35.

through evil entities under the direction and control of Satan, namely demons. Little more than a cursory glance at Christ's earthly healing ministry will lead us to conclude that the sicknesses of a significantly large proportion of those individuals, whom He healed, were caused by the presence of such demons.

During the inter-Testamental[43] period, a very sophisticated demonology had developed that attributed medical complaints – most often fever, acute malady and life-threatening ailments – to the presence of demons. These entities are variously described by the New Testament writers as 'evil spirits', 'unclean spirits' and 'spirits of infirmity'. We can safely conclude, therefore, that sickness and disease are major offensive weapons of Satan against humanity. Furthermore, Jesus of Nazareth did not dismiss the people's detection of demons as a mere primitive superstition, but rather He confronted the demons, who were already aware of His divine presence, before He rebuked and expelled them. In the biblical accounts of the blind and dumb demoniac, the gospel writers emphasise the connection between Jesus' healing exorcisms and the binding of the 'strong man', generally accepted by Bible scholars to be Satan. Referring to Luke's record of Jesus' vision of Satan falling from heaven like lightning,[44] Warrington states:

> Because of being set in the context of the exorcisms performed by the Seventy[45] it is probably better to see this as a reference to what took place

---

43. The period of approximately 400 years between the last prophecy of the Old Testament and the public ministry of John the Baptist and Jesus of Nazareth.
44. Luke 10:18.
45. Or seventy-two, according to some ancient manuscripts of Luke's gospel.

during those exorcisms; Satan was falling from his ascendancy in the lives of people as a result of the powerful intervention of the Kingdom of God.[46]

Since the prevailing Christian view is that Satan has fallen (at some point in the past) and that Christ has 'disarmed the powers and authorities, he made a public spectacle of them, triumphing over them by the cross' (Colossians 2:15) as a consequence of His incarnation and passion, we are likely to conclude like many Evangelicals that, unlike the time prior to Jesus' earthly ministry, it is presently impossible for a demon to attack or invade a human body with sickness. Yet despite this affirmation, we continue, in this present age, to see sickness and disease abound in all measure, including those strains and symptoms described by the gospel writers as having been specifically caused by an unclean spirit or a spirit of infirmity. Moreover, we see the apostles, after the death, resurrection and ascension of Christ, continuing to perform the same kinds of healing exorcisms as Christ Himself performed:

> The apostles performed many signs and wonders among the people. And all the believers used to meet together in Solomon's Colonnade. No one else dared join them, even though they were highly regarded by the people. Nevertheless, more and more men and women believed in the Lord and were added to their number. As a result, people brought those who were ill into the streets and laid them on beds and mats so that at least Peter's shadow might fall on some of them as he passed by. Crowds gathered also from the towns

---

46. Warrington, p.79.

around Jerusalem, bringing those who were ill and those tormented by impure spirits, and all of them were healed. (Acts 5:12-16)

Once when we were going to the place of prayer, we were met by a female slave who had[47] a spirit by which she predicted the future. She earned a great deal of money for her owners by fortune-telling. She followed Paul and the rest of us, shouting, 'These men are servants of the Most High God, who are telling you the way to be saved.' She kept this up for many days. Finally Paul became so annoyed that he turned round and said to the spirit, 'In the name of Jesus Christ I command you to come out of her!' At that moment the spirit left her. (Acts 16:16-18)

God did extraordinary miracles through Paul, so that even handkerchiefs and aprons that had touched him were taken to those who were ill, and their illnesses were cured and the evil spirits left them. Some Jews who went around driving out evil spirits tried to invoke the name of the Lord Jesus over those who were demon-possessed. They would say, 'In the name of Jesus whom Paul preaches, I command you to come out.' Seven sons of Sceva, a Jewish chief priest, were doing this. One day the evil spirit answered them, 'Jesus I know, and Paul I know about, but who are you?' Then the man who had the evil spirit jumped on them and overpowered them all. He gave them

---

47. Note: she had the spirit; the spirit didn't have her! See later comments on 'demon possession'.

such a beating that they ran out of the house naked and bleeding. (Acts 19:11-16)

If we, as a result of the strong biblical arguments in that direction, accept that some if not all illnesses are the specific result of demonic activity, it behoves us, as a topical argument, to define to what extent a Christian can be affected by such activity. Most Evangelical scholars will answer along the lines that Christians are not generally prone to it. One Evangelical writer who has long gone against this trend of thought on the subject is Neil T. Anderson. He writes generally as follows and not specifically with regard to illness:

> The fact that a Christian can be influenced by the 'god of this world' is a New Testament given. If not, why are we instructed to put on the whole armor of God and stand firm (Ephesians 6:10), to take every thought captive to the obedience of Christ (2 Corinthians 10:5) and to resist the devil (James 4:10)? And what if we don't? . . . We are easy prey for the enemy of our souls.[48]

While Anderson and the Freedom in Christ ministry which he has founded attribute mainly mental and social illnesses to the onslaught of demonic activity, many Charismatics, such as the late John Wimber, attribute a whole spectrum of illnesses to demons without those demons actually 'possessing' an individual. Dr Peter Masters refutes Wimber's 'proofs' that demons are the cause of such illnesses as dumbness, blindness, epilepsy, high fever and crippling. Masters cites the woman in Luke 13:10-17 who is said

---

48. Anderson, Dr Neil T., *Released From Bondage* (Tunbridge Wells: Monarch, 1993), p.16.

to have a spirit of infirmity, where there appears to be a demon at work, but without it actually possessing the person, as the only valid biblical argument backing Wimber's position:

> On a Sabbath Jesus was teaching in one of the synagogues, and a woman was there who had been *crippled by a spirit* for eighteen years. She was bent over and could not straighten up at all. When Jesus saw her, he called her forward and said to her, 'Woman, you are set free from your infirmity.' Then he put his hands on her, and immediately she straightened up and praised God. Indignant because Jesus had healed on the Sabbath, the synagogue leader said to the people, 'There are six days for work. So come and be healed on those days, not on the Sabbath.' The Lord answered him, 'You hypocrites! Doesn't each of you on the Sabbath untie your ox or donkey from the stall and lead it out to give it water? Then should not this woman, a daughter of Abraham, *whom Satan has kept bound* for eighteen long years, be set free on the Sabbath day from what bound her? (Emphasis added)

Masters is drawing what he believes to be a significant distinction, arguing that being bound by Satan is not the same as being possessed. This is a valid distinction to draw, however difficulty arises in this line of argument because of allegedly poor English translations. Anderson states: 'In the English translations the term "demon possession" is derived from only one Greek word. Therefore I prefer to use the word "demonised" instead.'[49] The rendering of people who are affected or influenced by demons as being 'demon possessed' is unhelpful, since it appears that the demon possesses or owns the person, whereas it *seems more evident that it is the person who possesses the demon.*[50] Masters nevertheless backtracks and states:

> However, it is fairly evident that this poor woman was demon possessed, for Jesus described her as one – *whom Satan hath bound.* She was a tied-up prisoner whose awful physical afflictions were a graphic manifestation and reflection of her deeper subjection to demonic captivity.[51]

Drawing this conclusion from the biblical text appears to require more licence than Wimber's exegesis does. Appearing to contradict his previous argument regarding the bent-over woman,[52] Masters goes on to state that:

> The only person in scripture whose illness was affected by a demon without there being 'full demon possession' was Job, but in this instance Satan had to ask God for specific permission to afflict him.[53]

The problem confronting many Reformed scholars is a theology of Satan that appears to seriously limit God's sovereignty. Gross cites C. Peter Wagner as one who allegedly supports this so-called limitation of God's sovereignty, quoting him thus:

---

49. Anderson, p.15.
50. See footnote #47.
51. Masters, p.85.
52. Note that she is described as a 'daughter of Abraham', i.e. a child of covenant relationship.
53. Masters, p.86.

> First of all, is sickness God's will? A good way to address that question is to raise another one. Is sickness a kingdom value? Obviously not . . . If sickness is not God's will, but many people in fact are sick, what is the cause? The answer clearly is Satan.[54]

We are still faced with the reality that if sickness and disease can be caused by the presence of a spirit of infirmity, and if one receives deliverance from all spirits at the point of conversion (the general position adopted by most Evangelicals), then improved health, we assume, would result immediately. Yet we rarely hear of any previously sick person who has received a dramatic and instant physical healing at the point of that person's conversion. It is taught unchallenged that sin in the life of the Christian is the result of yielding to temptation. Since God tempts no one, this temptation must be from Satan. If, however, it is suggested that the sickness from which a Christian may be suffering is from Satan, the suggestion is generally met with indignation among Evangelicals.

Much of the teaching of the Early Church Fathers took the influence of the devil in the life of the Christian much more seriously than the Church does today. Catechumens[55] were subjected to exorcism prior to their baptism, to remove demons that had the potential to lead them into post-baptismal sin.[56] Significantly, in those early days, demons were also regarded to be the cause of illness. Tertullian, to whom what we regard as orthodox theology owes much, records:

---

54. Wagner, C. Peter, *How to Have a Healing Ministry Without Making Your Church Sick* (Ventura, CA: Regal Books, 1988), p.109, cited in Gross, p.98.
55. I.e. those receiving instruction in preparation for Christian baptism or confirmation.
56. In the Early Church period, it was believed generally that 'serious' post-baptismal sin was potentially damning for the individual concerned.

> Many of our Christian men . . . have healed and
> do heal . . . driving the . . . demon out . . . though
> they could not be cured . . . by those who use
> incantations and drugs.[57]

Gross, who entirely rejects the concept of healing through deliverance from demons, surprisingly suggests that certain miraculous healings are actually the work of demonic deception! He nevertheless admits that the Bible clearly reveals demonic attacks upon Christians with varying results of ensuing success.[58] In support of the Christian's vulnerability to the demonic, C.S. Lewis writes of the two opposing errors we can fall into as human beings. One is to discount the possibility of evil spirits; the other is to be overly interested in them.[59]

When we conclude that sickness of various strains cannot be caused by a demon, we not only veer towards one of Lewis's extremes, but also the reference in 1 Corinthians 12 to a spiritual gift involving the individual's discerning of spirits is in danger of being rendered redundant.

There is undoubtedly a connection between Satan and sin, and we have discussed at some length the connection between Satan and sickness. The notion of a linkage between personal sin and sickness is a theological topic that is equally as divisive as the discussion on the extent to which demons can influence the Christian. It is nevertheless a clear Old Testament theme. Much of the content of the Levitical law recognises sickness and disease as the punishment for transgression. The context of the scripture that classical Pentecostals regard as key to

---

57. Penn-Lewis, Jessie, with Roberts, Evan, *War On the Saints* (New York, NY: Thomas E. Lowe, Ltd, 1984). Justin Martyr's second Apology, quoted p.314.
58. Gross, p.163.
59. Lewis, C.S., *The Screwtape Letters* (London: Fontana, 1955). See Preface, p.ix.

the Bible's teaching on divine healing, 'I am the LORD that healeth thee' (Exodus 15:26 KJV), refers to God's removal of the sicknesses caused by transgression, conditional upon personal forgiveness being sought[60] (in particular the illnesses that the sinful practices of the Egyptians had brought upon them). The same sequence may be captured in Psalm 103:3, 'He forgives all my sins and heals all my diseases' (NLT).[61]

It can be argued from Scripture that it is not just one's own personal sins that are capable of causing one to have illnesses, for the idea of vicarious suffering for ancestral sin is also evident in the Old Testament, where God resolved to visit the iniquities of the fathers upon their children (Exodus 20:5 KJV). This principle has a vivid illustration in

---

60. Although it is of interest that this verse immediately follows the healing of the bitter waters at Marah, suggesting a wide scope of healing in God's title beyond the diseases and afflictions of the human body.

61. We in the United Kingdom are very much a 'benefits society', each of us being very much aware of our state entitlements. How many Christians are fully aware of their Kingdom entitlements? 'Praise the Lord, O my soul, and forget not all his *benefits*' – Who:

   1. Forgives all your sins: 'He will not always accuse, nor will he harbour his anger for ever; he does not treat us as our sins deserve or repay us according to our iniquities. For as high as the heavens are above the earth, so great is his love for those who fear him; as far as the east is from the west, so far has he removed our transgressions from us' (vv.9-12).

   2. Heals all your diseases: 'He (the LORD) said, "If you listen carefully to the LORD your God and do what is right in his eyes, if you pay attention to his commands and keep all his decrees, I will not bring on you any of the diseases I brought on the Egyptians, for I am the LORD, who heals you' (Exodus 15:26).

   3. Redeems your life from the pit: 'He lifted me out of the slimy pit, out of the mud and mire; he set my feet on a rock and gave me a firm place to stand. He put a new song in my mouth, a hymn of praise to our God. Many will see and fear the LORD and put their trust in him' (Psalm 40:2-3).

   4. Crowns you with love and compassion: 'Blessed is the one who perseveres under trial, because, having stood the test, that person will receive the crown of life that the Lord has promised to those who love him' (James 1:12).

   5. Satisfies your desires with good things so that your youth is renewed like the eagle's: 'He gives strength to the weary and increases the power of the weak. Even youths grow tired and weary, and young men stumble and fall; but those who hope in the LORD will renew their strength. They will soar on wings like eagles; they will run and not grow weary, they will walk and not be faint' (Isaiah 40:29-31).

   Borrowed with permission from a sermon on Psalm 103 by Paul Bennison, a healing evangelist.

the life of King David. As a judgement for his sin of adultery with Bathsheba and the consequent shameful treatment and eventual murder of her 'mighty man'[62] husband Uriah, the prophet Nathan predicted, 'In every generation some of your descendants will die a violent death' (2 Samuel 12:10 GNT). This prophecy culminated in the violent death of the Ultimate Son of David at the hands of Roman executioners. And significantly in the context of the relationship between sin and sickness, Nathan went on to proclaim to David: 'The son born to you will die.'[63] Subsequently, the boy became very ill and died. It is with this Old Testament understanding of the law of sowing and reaping in mind that the disciples of Jesus asked Him in John 9:2: 'Who sinned, this man or his parents, that he was born blind?' Jesus' answer teaches unequivocally that sickness is not always the result of either personal or ancestral sin, but that in certain instances, through the sickness, God will in some way be glorified.[64] As previously cited, Job is a prime example of this fact.

We can nevertheless also see through the record of the earthly ministry of Jesus that it is implied that the onslaught of sickness and disease definitely *can* be the result of personal sin. After Jesus had healed the man at the Pool of Bethesda from a state of paralysis, He said to him: 'Stop sinning or something worse may happen to you'

---

62. We tend to think that this unfortunate couple was unknown to the king and that he spotted Bathsheba by accident – not so! Uriah is listed as one of David's trusted inner circle of 'mighty men', and Bathsheba may well have travelled in David's company for many years before he was formally crowned king and they subsequently became reacquainted.
63. Following on from above, see how the innocent infant son of David was sentenced to death for sins that were not his own – what a deeply moving, prophetic picture of the Ultimate 'Son of David' in the Atonement.
64. Particularly through the divine intervention that brings about the healing of an individual from that sickness.

(John 5:14 GNT). The same strain of teaching may be interpreted from the treatment of the paralytic in Matthew 9:2-7. 'Your sins are forgiven you' was the pronouncement made by Jesus before he said, 'Take up your bed and walk.' Was Jesus 'simply' drawing a reaction from the doubting bystanders and consequently demonstrating that He knew the musings of their hearts, ultimately demonstrating that healing and forgiveness belong together? Or did the man's sin, or at the very least the guilt of his sin, have to be dealt with initially before his affliction could be removed? This line of teaching is further endorsed by the traditional interpretation[65] of Paul in 1 Corinthians when he offers a warning to those who have partaken of the Lord's Supper without giving due respect to the Body of the Lord:[66] 'That is why many of you are weak and sick and some have even died' (1 Corinthians 11:30 NLT). Additionally, the classic healing passage in chapter 5 of the epistle of James would seem to indicate that a lack of result in the natural physical healing process can, on occasion, point to the possibility of un-confessed sin in the life of the sick person: 'And the prayer offered in faith will make the sick person well; the Lord will raise them up. If they have sinned, they will be forgiven' (James 5:15).

We have previously discussed how Paul's thorn in the flesh is generally considered to be a physical affliction or malady of some kind, but it is interesting to take note of how it is

---

65. See footnote #30 for an alternative interpretation of this passage.
66. There is nevertheless a theological tension here, for even those who were responsible for breaking the Lord's physical body were afforded the potential forgiveness through Jesus' prayer on the cross. The fact that many received that forgiveness is evident from Luke's record of the feast of Pentecost some seven weeks after the prayer was prayed, when in response to the preaching of Peter, thousands who were in attendance at the previous Jewish festival were 'cut to the heart' and repented and were converted. Is it the spiritual body of Christ, i.e. His Church, that is being wronged in this instance leading to such a severe judgement?

described: as 'a messenger [*angelos*] of Satan'. In any other context, the English translation of this phrase would be an 'angel of Satan' or a demon!

It is a biblical fact that God in His sovereignty uses Satan and his evil agents to bring about His purposes with relation to judgement, as it seems He did with King Saul:

> Now the Spirit of the LORD had departed from Saul, and an evil[67] spirit from the LORD tormented him. Saul's attendants said to him, 'See, an evil spirit from God is tormenting you. Let our lord command his servants here to search for someone who can play the lyre. He will play when the evil spirit from God comes on you, and you will feel better.' . . . David came to Saul and entered his service. Saul liked him very much, and David became one of his armour-bearers. Then Saul sent word to Jesse, saying, 'Allow David to remain in my service, for I am pleased with him.' Whenever the spirit from God came on Saul, David would take his lyre and play. Then relief would come to Saul; he would feel better, and the evil spirit would leave him.[68]
> (1 Samuel 16:14-16, 21-23)

God will unleash similar sovereign judgement at the end of the age:

> The fifth angel sounded his trumpet, and I saw a star that had fallen from the sky to the earth. The star was given the key to the shaft of the Abyss.

---

67. Or *injurious*.
68. Note the sequence: Saul feels better and then the spirit leaves – not the other way around!

When he opened the Abyss, smoke rose from it like the smoke from a gigantic furnace. The sun and sky were darkened by the smoke from the Abyss. And out of the smoke locusts came down on the earth and were given power like that of scorpions of the earth. They were told not to harm the grass of the earth or any plant or tree, but only those people who did not have the seal of God on their foreheads. They were not allowed to kill them but only to torture them for five months. And the agony they suffered was like that of the sting of a scorpion when it strikes. During those days men will seek death but will not find it; they will long to die, but death will elude them. The locusts looked like horses prepared for battle. On their heads they wore something like crowns of gold, and their faces resembled human faces. Their hair was like women's hair, and their teeth were like lions' teeth. They had breastplates like breastplates of iron, and the sound of their wings was like the thundering of many horses and chariots rushing into battle. They had tails and stings, like scorpions, and in their tails they had power to torment people for five months. They had as king over them the angel of the Abyss, whose name in Hebrew is Abaddon, and in Greek is Apollyon (that is, Destroyer). (Revelation 9:1-11)

Then I saw three *evil*[69] spirits that looked like frogs; they came out of the mouth of the dragon, out of the mouth of the beast and out of the

---

69. Or *unclean*.

mouth of the false prophet. They are spirits of demons performing miraculous signs, and they go out to the kings of the whole world, to gather them for the battle on the great day of God Almighty. (Revelation 16:13-14 NIV 1984, emphasis added)

Such judgement can be administered upon unbelievers, but also upon believers who have fallen into deliberate sin and apostasy.

In the light of the foregoing, it is important for us to consider the following questions:

i.   Is it possible that the presence of a spirit of infirmity might only leave the body of a Christian through individual appropriation or exorcism?

ii. Could this be an event apart from, and subsequent to, spiritual regeneration?

iii. Is it possible that in some instances such a spirit may be permitted to stay to maintain humility in the individual, as in the case of the apostle Paul, and that freedom may not be granted in the light of the sufficiency of God's grace?

If we accept this immediately preceding view of the origin and administration of sickness and disease, then it is evident that we will believe that such modes of suffering are not God's will for His people any more than sinful behaviour is. In many of our Church traditions, we regularly pray, 'Thy will be done on earth as it is in heaven.' The picture of heaven portrayed in Isaiah, John's Revelation and elsewhere in Scripture, is one of freedom from the 'old order' of things (which includes not only sin but also sickness) and where the tree of life produces crops of fruit and leaves 'for healing of the nations' (Revelation 22:2).

On this basis, our practical approach to Christian healing must be driven authoritatively: firstly, on an offensive basis against the demonic perpetrators of the illness; and, secondly, with certainty that healing, although not always immediate, is God's will for the Christian in every event of sickness.

Was Jesus Ever Sick?

The connection we have drawn between sin and sickness will necessarily prompt us to ask, and subsequently answer the question, 'Was Jesus ever sick?' We have concluded that sickness may result from a specific sin but that that is not always the case, so for many there is no theological reason why Jesus could not have been sick on occasion. In his book *Jesus: The Hidden Years,* Paul E. Brown states: 'If the family had any infectious disease we must not assume Jesus did not catch it – there is no sin in having flu!'[70] Jesus must have been a healthy individual, however, to embark on a 40-day fast and suffer no lasting damage. He did not survive this fast because He was God, but because He was a healthy man, freshly anointed by the Holy Spirit. In the next section, we will discuss how Jesus must have been in excellent health to endure His last thirty-six hours to the point of laying down His life, and how, through His passion, we see how He best empathises with the suffering of the symptoms of serious illness. There is a reason, however, that He may not have been susceptible to illness and infection as

---

70. Brown, Paul E., *Jesus: The Hidden Years* (Leominster: Day One Publications, 2017), p.23.

we are – His blood[71] was different! An old hymn, 'Not All the Blood of Beasts' by Isaac Watts (1674-1748), begins:

Not all the blood of beasts
On Jewish altars slain
Could give the guilty conscience peace
Or wash away the stain.

But Christ, the heavenly Lamb,
Takes all our sins away;
A sacrifice of nobler name
And *richer blood* than they.

This 'richer blood'[72] is not simply a theological metaphor – the testimony of Jesus of Nazareth was not consistent with His human forebear who said, 'I was shapen in iniquity; and in sin did my mother conceive me' (Psalm 51:5 KJV) because He had neither the hereditary guilt of original sin nor the hereditary capacity to commit sin, passed down to Him through His bloodline. According to the teaching of the Roman Catholic Church, the Immaculate Conception is the conception of the 'Blessed Virgin Mary' free from original sin by virtue of the foreseen merits of her son Jesus Christ. This doctrine was the result of a theological dilemma as to how Jesus could have been born sinless from a sinful mother. We now know that the placental circulation brings into close relationship two circulation

---

71. 1 Peter 1:19 speaks of the 'precious blood'.
72. Hebrews 9:11-14: 'But when Christ came as high priest of the good things that are now already here, he went through the greater and more perfect tabernacle that is not made with human hands, that is to say, is not a part of this creation. He did not enter by means of the blood of goats and calves; but he entered the Most Holy Place once for all *by his own blood*, so obtaining eternal redemption. The blood of goats and bulls and the ashes of a heifer sprinkled on those who are ceremonially unclean sanctify them so that they are outwardly clean. How much more, then, will the blood of Christ, who through the eternal Spirit offered himself unblemished to God, cleanse our consciences from acts that lead to death, so that we may serve the living God!'

systems: the *maternal* and the *fetal*. The fetal blood supply comes entirely from the father. So Jesus of Nazareth's blood was entirely from His Father through His conception by the Holy Spirit.

In a first pregnancy, however, *these systems never mix*. Jesus' blood could have been influenced by Mary's lifestyle through the passing of essential nutrients from her blood stream through the placenta but could not have been contaminated by the passing of original sin in the blood stream. So Jesus may have been uniquely immune to many of the infections and diseases of His time. However, we need to balance how, when in compassion He touched highly infectious people such as lepers, that it was not simply as a consequence of His being immune to disease, meaning He could do so without risk.

It is also important to note that the New Testament scriptures do not deny that committed Christians may get sick from time to time, as was the case with Trophimus,[73] Epaphroditus,[74] Timothy[75] and perhaps Paul sporadically, as noted above, but they do seem to assure that healing and recovery are available on each occasion.

We have come to a clear understanding, through the arguments in this section, that the suffering caused by sickness appears to be in a different and unique category from the other forms of suffering to which the Christian is

---

73. 'I left Trophimus ill in Miletus' (2 Timothy 4:20).
74. 'But I think it is necessary to send back to you Epaphroditus, my brother, co-worker and fellow soldier, who is also your messenger, whom you sent to take care of my needs. For he longs for all of you and is distressed because you heard he was ill. Indeed he was ill, and almost died. But God had mercy on him, and not on him only but also on me, to spare me sorrow upon sorrow' (Philippians 2:25-27).
75. 'Stop drinking only water, and use a little wine because of your stomach and your frequent illnesses' (1 Timothy 5:23).

specifically called and is indeed expected to endure. Many believe that the reason that Christians have the right to claim their healing is because it has been purchased for them, just as their salvation has, through the Atonement of Christ.

Healing in the Atonement

For much of the history of the Church, the debate on the scope of the Atonement has almost always dealt with the question of whether or not Christ died for the sins of the whole of mankind, or for the sins of the elect only. The doctrine of 'Unlimited Atonement' or 'general redemption' (because God did not limit Christ's redemptive death to the elect) argues that the death of Christ was designed to atone for all mankind, whether or not all believe. To those who believe for salvation, Atonement is applied and, for those who do not believe, it provides the benefits of common grace[76] and also removes any excuse for being ultimately lost. This view is commonly referred to by theologians as 'Arminianism' after James Arminius who promoted the belief. Calvinism, on the other hand, based on the teaching of the Reformer John Calvin, holds to a doctrine of a 'Limited Atonement' – that God has limited the benefits available from Christ's death to a known, finite number of elect persons who will persevere to eternal life.

As a result of the rise of Pentecostalism and, more recently, the Charismatic or neo-Pentecostal movement, with a significant emphasis on Christian healing, considerable debate has emerged as to the general scope as opposed to

---

76. Common grace: undeserved blessings which God extends to all mankind in contrast to 'Special Grace' by which God redeems, sanctifies, and glorifies His people, according to Reformation teaching.

the individual scope of the Atonement. Proof of the lack of theological thought as to how healing should be understood with regard to the Atonement throughout much of the history of the Church is offered by the lack of reference to the subject in the 'classic' volumes of systematic theology and, until recently, the lack of systematic theologians with a Pentecostal or neo-Pentecostal persuasion. One of the first writers to contemplate a theology of healing which necessarily dealt with healing in the Atonement was Dr A.J. Gordon in his book *The Ministry of Healing*. In this work, Gordon cites Matthew 8:17:

> When evening came, many who were demon-possessed were brought to him, and he drove out the spirits with a word and healed all the sick. This was to fulfil what was spoken through the prophet Isaiah: 'He took up our infirmities and carried our diseases.'

Upon this passage, Gordon poses the premise, 'In the atonement of Christ there seems to be a foundation laid for faith in bodily healing.'[77] Rowland V. Bingham says of Gordon: 'It was the dogmatic assertion by later teachers of what he [Gordon] wrote suggestively and enquiringly, that brought this whole matter into question and led to a mistaken doctrine regarding it.' Dr T.J. McCrossan, who described himself as a 'Scotch-Canadian',[78] was one such later teacher whose 1930 work *Bodily Healing and the Atonement* was re-edited by Dr Roy Hicks and Dr Kenneth Hagin in 1982, and explains the basic scriptural premises for the doctrine. P.G. Chappell, a contemporary scholar,

---

77. Bingham, Rowland V., *The Bible and the Body* (Toronto: Evangelical Publishers, 1921). Bingham quotes Gordon on p.17.
78. And interestingly, was a Presbyterian clergyman.

whose PhD dissertation 'The Divine Healing Movement in America' (Drew University) states: 'The most controversial theological aspect of divine healing is its relationship to the Atonement.'[79] It is important to examine this relationship, not simply to understand what Pentecostal denominations believe together with the validity of that belief based on Scripture, but also to understand how a *Charismatic* view of divine healing can be reconciled with the doctrines of the various mainstream denominations, both Calvinistic and Arminian, where many Charismatics are in fellowship.

The traditional view of divine healing is that God heals whomever He wills whenever He wills, whereas the classical Pentecostal view holds that when Christ was scourged, He took upon Himself all our sicknesses and diseases so that by exercising faith we can be healed from every sickness and disease.

Most supporters of the continuance of the spiritual gift of healing as the means by which Christians receive or claim their healing (and which will be explained in detail in a later section of this work) believe that physical healing, like salvation, is an inheritance of every Christian through the passion and atoning death of Christ. This view uses the previously cited verses in Matthew 8 to interpret Isaiah 53:4-5:

> Surely he took up our pain and bore our suffering, yet we considered him punished by God, stricken by him, and afflicted. But he was pierced for our transgressions, he was crushed for our iniquities;

---

79. Elwell, W.A., ed., *Evangelical Dictionary of Theology* (Carlisle: Paternoster, 1995), p.498.

the punishment that brought us peace was on him, *and by his wounds we are healed. (Emphasis added)*

Therefore, it is possible to conclude that Christ bore man's bodily suffering in addition to his spiritual suffering through His passion. Thus, one receives one's physical healing by faith, just as one receives one's spiritual salvation. Two ideas exist as to how this healing can be received. The first idea is that through conversion, we are automatically physically healed through the scope of the Atonement. This idea is the basis for the concept that Christian health and salvation belong together and leaves no room for sickness post-conversion, other than as a result of personal sin. We also discussed earlier that:

i. Few individuals report full physical healing at the point of conversion; and

ii. Christians from the New Testament era and throughout Church history, right up until today, have got sick without there having been any indication of deliberate sin in their lives.

The second and more plausible idea is based on the belief that healing is appropriated and received also by faith, but independent of salvation, and on any occasion where an individual has become inevitably (by the standards of this idea) sick. Thus, in any event of illness, healing is received as an act of the individual's faith and will.

It is important to examine how well grounded the basis of each of these ideas is in Scripture, particularly the key passages in Isaiah 53. Matthew's citation of Isaiah 53:4

from the Septuagint[80] is rendered in the NIV: 'He took up our infirmities and carried our diseases.' Whereas the NIV translation of Isaiah 53:4, based on the Hebrew manuscripts, reads: 'He took up our infirmities and carries our sorrows.' While most contemporary scholars agree that the concept of a suffering Messiah would not have been consistent with Jewish teaching at the time of Matthew's writing, almost all are in agreement that the 'Suffering Servant' of Isaiah 53 provides a prophetic picture of the trial, sentencing and death of Jesus of Nazareth. Interestingly, Matthew seems to imply that Jesus had fulfilled the prophecy of Isaiah 53:4 during His life rather than as a result of His death. This may be an interpretation comfortable to non-Pentecostals, but it is with the benefit of the hindsight of Christ's death and resurrection that Matthew is writing his gospel. Also, compare the accounts of Christ forgiving sin prior to His death, as with the paralytic in Mark 2:5, the sinful woman in Luke 7:48, and as implied in the account of the woman taken in adultery in John 8:10. In the case of the healing of the paralytic in Mark 2:5, Christ exercised His authority on earth to forgive sins prior to the event whereby the atonement for those sins actually took place, i.e. His crucifixion and consequent death.

A study of the available Hebrew text certainly does identify the Servant of Isaiah 53 with more than the affliction caused by torture and execution at the hands of men. For example, verse 3 has been translated, 'A man of sorrows, familiar with sickness' (NASB). It is nevertheless verse 5, 'And with his stripes we are healed' (KJV), that is cited most often with regard to healing in the Atonement. These

---

80. This Greek translation of the Old Testament was the Bible of Jesus of Nazareth and His first disciples.

scriptures are quoted based on the understanding that it was during the flogging that Christ endured, prior to His crucifixion, that He atoned for sickness, disease and pain. McCrossan points out that the verbs to 'take up' (NIV) or to 'bear' and 'carry' (KJV), *nasa* and *salal* respectively, are used elsewhere for the vicarious bearing of sins and the bearing of a chastisement or penalty.[81] Although not plainly evident from any of the literature studied in the preparation of this work, it is known to be popular pulpit teaching by Pentecostals that there are thirty-nine major strains of disease and sickness in the world, and on the basis of the tradition that He received thirty-nine lashes from the Roman scourge, it is accepted that Christ atoned for each one of these strains.

It is, however, on the cross that we see the climax of Christ's physical suffering and where He seemingly best empathises with the suffering of the symptoms of serious illness. The conditions of helplessness, loneliness, dehydration, organ failure, fluid in the lungs, loss of bodily control,[82] loss of dignity, confusion and intensity of pain that normally requires drugging, were all at once experienced by God incarnate. If we were to judge the Atonement solely on the basis of our understanding of a sacrifice, then in the light of the Levitical law, Christ's death as a sacrifice for sin (however undeserved because of His sinless life) *could have and should have entailed a humane execution.* No sacrificial animal of the ceremonial law was made to suffer unduly prior to its death. There appeared to be a divine necessity to extend Christ's Atonement 'package' beyond

---

81. McCrossan, p.12.
82. Although not generally contemplated, most likely double incontinence, due to the stress, pain and weakness caused by the mode of execution and, of course, the law of gravity.

that assumed by the Old Testament understanding of a substitutionary atonement for sin. Baptist minister Herbert Carson, who is neither Pentecostal nor Charismatic, states by way of explanation, 'Thus Jesus the suffering servant of the Lord, bore our guilt and our liability to condemnation, and at the same time bore our sicknesses, which are the outward element of our fallen state.' Furthermore, he makes the point, 'The cross had not only implications in the area of personal sin, but had further reference to sickness and death, and indeed has cosmic significance in that it purchased the deliverance of the created order from the sorry entail of the fall.' Carson nevertheless rejects that all Christians have the right to healing and health on the basis of Christ's work of atonement any more than they have a right to sinless perfection in this life.[83]

Another popular text for the advocates of divine healing through the Atonement is the previously cited text of Psalm 103:3.[84] In the context of praising God for all His benefits, the psalmist begins to list those benefits: 'Who forgives all your sins and heals all your diseases.' We note here that the psalmist assimilates the forgiveness of sin rather than the enabling of a sinless life with the healing of diseases, undermining Carson's point stated earlier. It is nevertheless reasonable to assume that on the cross, Christ purchased mankind's entrance to a Kingdom where not only sin but also sickness, sorrow and suffering of all kinds will ultimately be banished, as will the last scourge of sin – that of death itself. In a case where a miraculous healing has taken place, we experience the first fruits of

83. Carson, Herbert, *Spiritual Gifts for Today?* (Eastbourne: Kingsway, 1987), p.101.
84. Gaebelein, A.C., *The Healing Question* (New York, NY: Our Hope, 1925), p.132. Gaebelein regards this psalm as speaking of the 'Future Kingdom'. It is hard to reconcile this view with the later references to man's frailty (vv.14-16).

that Kingdom: a foretaste for some, prior to the eternal reality of these events. As long as the Christian retains a mortal body, that body will be prone to sickness, disease and pain. However, at the resurrection when the person is raised with what the apostle Paul refers to as an incorruptible body, these temporal problems will no longer affect that body because of what Christ accomplished through His Atonement. Alban Douglas argues against us reaching the conclusion that healing is included in the Atonement and states: 'If healing is in the Atonement, both salvation and healing would be eternal. But history proves that even the best saints have to die.'[85] This, however, is a contradiction, for even though the punishment for sin that is deserved by 'the best saints' has been dealt with in the Atonement, and 'the wages of sin is death', those same saints still have to die.

If we consider the Atonement as a victory, particularly a victory over Satan who, in a previous section, we identified and portrayed as the originator and administrator of sickness and disease, we can see very clearly how reasonable it is for healing to be a crucial element of that Atonement. If Christ waged war against these emissaries of Satan during His earthly ministry, how much more likely it is to conclude that, as previously cited, when He 'disarmed the powers and authorities, he made a public spectacle of them, triumphing over them by the cross' (Colossians 2:15), that such a victory, of necessity, incorporated the defeat of the effects of sickness and disease whose origins and inflictions we have argued are diabolical?

---

85.   Douglas, p.202.

In considering healing as part of the Atonement, a significant dilemma faces us in dealing with the healing of unbelievers. Many at the time of Jesus' earthly ministry, in the post-apostolic period of Church history and no doubt in the present time, have experienced healing as the result of the prayers of Christians or as a result of the Christian gift of healing but have not professed Christian faith for salvation either prior to the healing or as a result of it. Of the ten lepers healed by Jesus, only one returned to give thanks. In many instances both now and then, the healing miracle led to spiritual conversion, as seemed to be the case of the paralytic in Mark 2 and the blind man of John 9:

> Jesus heard that they had thrown him [the man born blind] out, and when he found him, he said, 'Do you believe in the Son of Man?' 'Who is he, sir?' the man asked. 'Tell me so that I may believe in him.' Jesus said, 'You have now seen him; in fact, he is the one speaking with you.' Then the man said, 'Lord, I believe,' and he worshipped him. (John 9:35-38)

In other cases, however, we have no evidence that this was so,[86] therefore in such instances we may assume it is the exercising of faith by other Christians or by the one administering the healing that brings about the miracle, as opposed to the individual faith of the beneficiary of the healing. Holding to the Pentecostal view, these miracles of healing must have been accomplished through the

---

86. In fact, the rather small number that constituted the body of believers on the Day of Pentecost (120) was in stark contrast to the multitudes healed by Jesus and the disciples over the period of their three-year ministry.

Atonement. While this analysis is consistent with a 'general redemption' view of the Atonement, i.e. that Christ suffered universally for sin and in this case universally for sickness (and this would be the theological standpoint of most Pentecostal denominations), it does not explain why, on occasion, unbelievers are healed and many believing church members are not. Perhaps a 'Calvinist' approach is more adequate in that, if Christ atoned only for the sins of those elected to be saved, perhaps He further atoned only for the healing of those elected to be healed, a group not equating to, but overlapping with, the first group.[87] The best explanation, however, may lie in the fact that according to the evidence of Scripture, divine healing can seemingly be administered vicariously, i.e. through the faith of those other than the recipient of that healing. The person who exercises such faith may be the parent of the sick person, as in the case of the epileptic boy (Mark 9:14-26); a friend or friends, as in the healing of the paralytic (Mark 2:1-5); an employer, as in the case of the centurion's servant (Matthew 8:5-13); an elder (James 5:13-16) as well as the recipient (Mark 5:25-34). Personal salvation, by contrast, must always be appropriated by individual, personal faith. *Thus it can be postulated that Jesus Christ atoned for all sin and all sickness, and that the benefits can be drawn upon through faith: individual faith for salvation and individual or vicarious faith,[88] if necessary, for healing.*

---

87. A further problem arises from the teaching of the late 19th-century Holiness Movement. A.B. Simpson, originator of the Christian and Missionary Alliance, writes of divine healing: 'It is a gift of grace, as all that Christ's blood has purchased will ever be, and therefore cannot be mixed up with our own works or the use of human means.' This effectively bans all medical and surgical treatment for the Christian as human attempts to add to grace. (Simpson, quoted in Bingham, p.53.)
88. The part that faith plays in healing is discussed in greater depth later in this work.

If we believe that healing is contained in the Atonement and therefore is the right of every Christian believer, it will significantly influence how we practise our healing ministry and will ultimately stimulate the expectation of a 100 per cent success rate.

Does God Deal With Injuries in a Different Way From Sicknesses and Diseases?

If Jesus suffered in the way described in the earlier section, that is, by way of injury rather than by the symptoms of a disease, it should then follow that our bodily injuries, whether inflicted accidentally or intentionally, should also be catered for by His Atonement. The author records in his journal:

> I remember some years ago coming upon a road traffic accident involving a car and a truck. The car had gone underneath part of the rear of the truck thereby compressing the car roof onto the head of its driver. Before the emergency services arrived, quite a crowd had gathered. I felt led to break through and lay hands on the unconscious man and claim his healing. I have no idea what the outcome of my action was and I never heard another thing about the accident. I was sure that I had done what Jesus would have done but was unable to think of any event recorded in the gospels where He had healed an injury as opposed to a sickness or disease.

The author is sure that the lepers that Jesus healed had had bodily injuries caused by the onset of the disease, and that these were healed at the same time as the disease. Prior to his deliverance, the man formerly known as Legion had the physical injuries resulting from his demon-instigated actions.[89] When he was healed by Jesus, he was rendered 'clothed and in his right mind', but we can envisage how his bodily injuries ('Night and day among the tombs and in the hills he would cry out and cut himself with stones' [Mark 5:5]) may also have been healed simultaneously. However, it is the book of Acts that comes to our rescue. When Paul and a missionary entourage that included Luke, the author of the book,[90] were en route to Jerusalem, they stopped off at Troas.

> On the first day of the week we came together to break bread. Paul spoke to the people and, because he intended to leave the next day, kept on talking until midnight. There were many lamps in the upstairs room where we were meeting. Seated in a window was a young man named Eutychus, who was sinking into a deep sleep as Paul talked on and on. When he was sound asleep, he fell to the ground from the third storey and was picked up dead. Paul went down, threw himself on the young man and put his arms around him. 'Don't be alarmed,' he said. 'He's alive!' Then he went upstairs again and broke bread and ate. After talking until daylight, he left. The people took the young man home alive and were greatly comforted. (Acts 20:7-12)

Clearly, there was no disease involved and the fatal injuries were healed!

---

89. In the author's experience, there is often a clear link between self-harm and demonic influence.
90. Note the narrative has switched to the first person in this chapter.

How Does God Heal?

This may seem a strange question to ask. Does it matter how, as long as He does heal? The question nevertheless needs answering in some measure if we are to press forward into a better understanding of what may seem to be a present-day failure on the part of the Almighty or, at least, His followers. It is also true that God is sovereign and can choose to do what He desires, in any way that He desires. However, God is a God of order and therefore of process. He could have snapped His fingers and the world would have come into being, yet He chose to use a process, a process that Christians are still trying to understand in the light of reason and scientific discovery. He chose to execute that process over a period of six days (however we interpret the scope and duration of those days) according to His word, with each day having an order and a degree of logic. When we make plans and use orderly processes in our lives, and to accomplish our work, it is because we have been made in the image of an orderly Creator. It seems that God is orderly in all that He does, including in His acts of healing.

God heals naturally – The significance of this is often overlooked, but God has clearly demonstrated His desire for wholeness in His creation together with His willingness to heal us, in the way that He has made us. As the psalmist tells us, we are 'fearfully and wonderfully made' (Psalm 139:14); if we cut our skin, break a bone, contract a virus, get a sick stomach or a cold, take a blow that causes a bruise, sprain a joint or are struck down by any number of minor diseases, the natural outcome is that after a predictable period of time we will recover. 'Time is the healer,' we say; even emotional illnesses and the pain of bereavement subside with the passage of time. We are regenerative by nature, hence we brand chronic ailments that resist the body's tendency to renew itself and to alleviate the symptoms as 'degenerative'.

God heals as the Author of time – In view of the natural tendency to regain health as time passes, it is not surprising that in a case of miraculous healing, the Author of time should suspend the natural laws of time local to an individual's body and speed up the natural healing process by speeding up time. This is most likely the method of healing used by Jesus Christ in the account of the miraculous recovery of Peter's mother-in-law:

> As soon as they left the synagogue, they went with James and John to the home of Simon and Andrew. Simon's mother-in-law was in bed with a fever, and they immediately told Jesus about her. So he went to her, took her hand and helped her up. The fever left her and she began to wait on them. (Mark 1:29-31)

There is no indication that this was a serious ailment. Most Bible scholars reckon it was a heavy cold or virus that this lady was suffering from. There is no reason to believe that, given time, Peter's mother-in-law would not have made a full recovery. Jesus did not have time to spare on this occasion, however. 'While it was day', He resolved to do the will of His Father. Humanly speaking, He was tired and hungry and the presence of this fever was an inconvenience to Him and His ministry, as well as a source of suffering to Peter's mother-in-law. There is also a hint here at the diabolical nature of sickness which regularly hampers the work of God's children as they seek to extend His Kingdom and render acts of hospitality. Jesus, it seems, simply speeded up time local to this woman's body until the natural healing process made her strong and well and available.

If the Author of time can speed up time to fulfil His purposes, then it follows that He can move time backwards on a localised or individual basis. In the healing of degenerative illnesses, there is a need for the effects of various unhealthy conditions to be reversed. It is unthinkable that the poor lepers whom Jesus healed continued on with limbs damaged and missing. The restoration that took place must have resembled a turning back of the clock.

The author has recorded his personal experience as follows:

> On my first trip to Cali, Colombia, I was asked to speak at one of the Sunday morning services. As we celebrated during the praise time a man began to dance at the front of the church. He grabbed me, a celebrated non-dancer, and we swayed without rhythm for a short while. After the service, when prayer ministry was offered, the man took a shoe and sock off and revealed that one of his impediments to rhythmic dancing was a missing toe on one foot. His request was simple: a new toe!

Consider the Old Testament account of Namaan's healing from leprosy:

> So Naaman went with his horses and chariots and stopped at the door of Elisha's house. Elisha sent a messenger to say to him, 'Go, wash yourself

seven times in the Jordan, and your flesh will be restored and you will be cleansed.' But Naaman went away angry and said, 'I thought that he would surely come out to me and stand and call on the name of the LORD his God, wave his hand over the spot and cure me of my leprosy. Are not Abana and Pharpar, the rivers of Damascus, better than any of the waters of Israel? Couldn't I wash in them and be cleansed?' So he turned and went off in a rage. Naaman's servants went to him and said, 'My father, if the prophet had told you to do some great thing, would you not have done it? How much more, then, when he tells you, "Wash and be cleansed"!' So he went down and dipped himself in the Jordan seven times, as the man of God had told him, and his flesh was restored and became clean *like that of a young boy*. (2 Kings 5:9-14, emphasis added)

What young boy did Namaan's flesh become like? The skin of the young Namaan presumably!

If Namaan or any of the lepers whom Jesus healed had, like the man from Cali, been missing a toe as the result of this disease, would not a reversal of time local to the sufferer's body have been the key to restoration? Would not the restoration of the toe have been our expectation in the numerous biblical accounts of leprosy being cured? Should we be surprised that someone in this day and age would have the same expectation?

Another good illustration of the time-reversal process is recorded in the account of an Old Testament healing; the healing of Hezekiah from a fatal illness. This appears to be a particularly important account as it is the only healing outside of the New Testament that is recorded in triplicate (2 Kings 20, 2 Chronicles 32 and Isaiah 38).

> In those days Hezekiah became ill and was at the point of death. The prophet Isaiah son of Amoz went to him and said, 'This is what the LORD says: put your house in order, because you are going to die; you will not recover.' Hezekiah turned his face to the wall and prayed to the LORD, 'Remember, LORD, how I have walked before you faithfully and with wholehearted devotion and have done what is good in your eyes.' And Hezekiah wept bitterly. Before Isaiah had left the middle court, the word of the LORD came to him: 'Go back and tell Hezekiah, the ruler of my people, "This is what the LORD, the God of your father David, says: I have heard your prayer and seen your tears; I will heal you. On the third day from now you will go up to the temple of the LORD. I will add fifteen years to your life. And I will deliver you and this city from the hand of the king of Assyria. I will defend this city for my sake and for the sake of my servant David."' Then Isaiah said, 'Prepare a poultice of figs.' They did so and applied it to the boil, and he recovered. Hezekiah had asked Isaiah, 'What will be the sign that the LORD will heal me and that I will go up to the temple of the LORD on the third day from now?' Isaiah answered, 'This is the LORD's sign to you that the LORD will do what he has promised: shall the shadow go forward ten steps, or shall it go back ten steps?' 'It is a simple matter for the shadow to go forward ten steps,'

said Hezekiah. 'Rather, let it go back ten steps.' Then the prophet Isaiah called upon the LORD, and the LORD made the shadow go back the ten steps it had gone down on the stairway of Ahaz. (2 Kings 20:1-11)

Bearing in mind that the sun was the only reliable and practical means of measuring the passage of time in that primitive age, the fact of time going backwards – albeit for a short while – may demonstrate the means by which Hezekiah was healed by the Lord. Might He have dialled back the timeline of Hezekiah's life by fifteen years and restored his diseased body to the healthy condition it had previously been in?

The healing testimony of someone you know is always effective. With his permission to include it, Brian Scott from West Church tells his story:

In 1958, while in the Merchant Navy, I injured my back and spent some time in hospital. Following my discharge from hospital I returned to work but thereafter I had trouble with my back, having spells of back pain lasting for weeks at a time. Between these attacks I was well and had no pain at all. However, over the years the attacks became more frequent and often I would not only have pain, but also a 'twist' in my back which pulled me over to one side. I was advised to put a board under my mattress, but usually I had most ease when lying on the floor.

Over the past 20 years I attended the late Dr George Gregg in the Royal Victoria Hospital on many occasions. Dr Gregg died about 5 years ago and I was concerned as to whom I should see if the problem arose again. However, about that time my wife was asked to a prayer and praise meeting in West Church, which she very much enjoyed, and eventually we started to go to the praise services on a Sunday evening.

In 1983 we moved from Gilnahirk to Dundonald and we needed a new path in the garden. Feeling fairly fit at the time, I decided to do the job myself with the help of a friend. However, shortly afterwards I again developed back pain with severe pain radiating down my left leg to the foot. I tried lying in bed for a few days but had no ease from this, so I decided to go back to work with the aid of a walking stick. I went to see my own doctor and received pain-relieving tablets and anti-inflammatory tablets, but unfortunately these didn't help. Weeks went past and I was in continuous pain.

One Sunday evening my wife wanted to take her mother to the praise service in West. My back was extremely painful but I felt I wanted to go to the service with them. When we got into the church I found it very difficult to sit on the wooden chairs and Anne asked me if I would like to go home. However, I felt I wanted to stay. I had to pull myself up out of the chair by holding on to the chair in front of me when we had to stand for the hymns. When Mr Bailie made the announcements, he mentioned the healing service and my wife asked me if I wouldn't like to go to that service. I felt it would be rather long for my wife, mother-in-law, and son to hang around, but they persuaded me. I was very thankful when the main service ended as I was very sore indeed, and on entering the Praise Room where the healing service is held, I just propped myself against the wall as I couldn't possibly sit down again.

Mr Bailie came over to speak to me and William Hall was with him. Mr Bailie put his hand on my shoulder and William prayed. I felt movement in my back which I can only describe as like a venetian blind closing, or a row of dominoes toppling over. The pain was disappearing, and I was able to raise my left foot from the floor quite easily. By the time the prayer was over I was completely free of pain.

It was a wonderful feeling to be free of pain and I thanked God for healing me and then I spoke to Mr Bailie and William. Following this I was able to drive my mother-in-law across town without any pain whatsoever. Since that day, now 3 years ago, I have never had pain in my back or down my leg. The Great Physician had healed me and I now know from personal experience that miracles do still happen today, just as they did 2,000 years ago.

POST-SCRIPT August 2003

Following my healing I asked God to show me what He wanted me to do for Him. I continued to pray for guidance as I did not feel led in any particular direction, but sometimes the answer is so simple we just don't see it. I was a technical representative and travelled all over Northern Ireland and I often found myself telling people about my healing. One day I realised that God was using me and I just hadn't been aware of it. I had called to see an engineer who was having a problem with a machine in a big engineering company. During the course of our conversation, he mentioned that he had a 'bad back' and was in considerable pain. I asked him if he'd had prayer for his condition, and he said it was the only thing he hadn't tried. I then told him of my healing, which he thought was an amazing experience. I then opened my briefcase and gave him one on my testimony sheets which I always carried for just such a situation. This made me realise just how God was using me in my everyday business, to glorify His name.

When I look back over my life I see how God has been with me all the way and I want to continue serving Him. Because of this healing I am particularly thrilled to be able to assist the Special Care Group with the disabled children – something I most certainly could not have done before the Lord healed me.

The ultimate reversal of time is, of course, the healing of Lazarus:

On his arrival, Jesus found that Lazarus had already been in the tomb for four days. Now

Bethany was less than two miles from Jerusalem, and many Jews had come to Martha and Mary to comfort them in the loss of their brother. When Martha heard that Jesus was coming, she went out to meet him, but Mary stayed at home. 'Lord,' Martha said to Jesus, 'if you had been here, my brother would not have died. But I know that even now God will give you whatever you ask.' Jesus said to her, 'Your brother will rise again.' Martha answered, 'I know he will rise again in the resurrection at the last day.' Jesus said to her, 'I am the resurrection and the life. The one who believes in me will live, even though they die; and whoever lives by believing in me will never die. Do you believe this?' 'Yes, Lord,' she told him, 'I believe that you are the Messiah, the Son of God, who is to come into the world.' After she had said this, she went back and called her sister Mary aside. 'The Teacher is here,' she said, 'and is asking for you.' When Mary heard this, she got up quickly and went to him. Now Jesus had not yet entered the village, but was still at the place where Martha had met him. When the Jews who had been with Mary in the house, comforting her, noticed how quickly she got up and went out, they followed her, supposing she was going to the tomb to mourn there. When Mary reached the place where Jesus was and saw him, she fell at his feet and said, 'Lord, if you had been here, my brother would not have died.' When Jesus saw her weeping, and the Jews who had come along with her also weeping, he was deeply moved in spirit and troubled. 'Where have you laid him?'

he asked. 'Come and see, Lord,' they replied. Jesus wept. Then the Jews said, 'See how he loved him!' But some of them said, 'Could not he who opened the eyes of the blind man have kept this man from dying?' Jesus, once more deeply moved, came to the tomb. It was a cave with a stone laid across the entrance. 'Take away the stone,' he said. 'But, Lord,' said Martha, the sister of the dead man, 'by this time there is a bad odour, for *he has been there four days.*' Then Jesus said, 'Did I not tell you that if you believe, you will see the glory of God?' So they took away the stone. Then Jesus looked up and said, 'Father, I thank you that you have heard me. I knew that you always hear me, but I said this for the benefit of the people standing here, that they may believe that you sent me.' When he had said this, Jesus called in a loud voice, 'Lazarus, come out!' The dead man came out, his hands and feet wrapped with strips of linen, and a cloth round his face. Jesus said to them, 'Take off the grave clothes and let him go.' (John 11:17-43, emphasis added)

At this point, Lazarus's personal time clock was reversed to a point when he was alive, apparently a time before he succumbed to his fatal illness, since it appeared that no further healing ministry or medication was required. In the next chronological reference in Scripture that we have to Lazarus, he is apparently in good health, sharing a meal in Jesus' honour (John 12:2).

God performs divine surgery – In order to heal, God may need to remove diseased organs. At this point, the author will share from his journal a personal testimony of God's healing in his own life:

> I recall clearly the year we were married how I had been plagued by an inflamed throat that was accompanied by what I can only describe as a permanent strain of the vocal muscles. As well as having the regular feeling of choking and of having an obstruction, my voice was regularly hoarse. Several visits to my doctor had led him to conclude that the tonsillitis I had had as a child had recurred and that the only permanent answer to my problem was for me to have my tonsils removed. This problem had persisted for two years when we were invited to a special praise and ministry weekend in a local Pentecostal church. The visiting worship band led us in a song whose origin I have never been able to trace. These are some of the words:
>
> > I will offer up a sacrifice to You
> > Expressing praise,
> > Because Your word Is true.
> > And I will bless Your name
> > No matter what I'm going through,
> > Yes, I will offer up a sacrifice to You . . .
> > I will offer up a sacrifice of praise
> > Although I may not feel
> > I have a reason to rejoice.
> > It's not a sacrifice,
> > Until you pay the price,
> > And I've made my choice,
> > I will lift my voice.

That night as we sang the 'Eight-fold Alleluia' I was aware of making a painful vocal sacrifice[91] (painful, perhaps, for the people standing next to me in the meeting as well!). But I knew as I worshipped that God was going to heal my condition. It did not happen that night, but I was able to cancel the tonsillectomy, which I was on a waiting list for, some while later. Many years afterwards I was having a routine medical examination by the company doctor in the firm where I worked, as a condition of my corporate medical insurance. The subject of my prior inflamed tonsils was discussed. 'You obviously had the surgery,' the doctor said, 'because you don't have any tonsils now'! Is it possible that God the Healer performed divine surgery upon me? It is entirely possible.

---

91. Worship is always accompanied by sacrifice in the Old Testament. The first mention of worship in the Old Testament is found in the account of God's testing of Abraham in Genesis chapter 22. He told his servants to stay with the asses while he and Isaac went to worship. To Abraham, the sacrifice was the offering up of his beloved son Isaac – a costly presentation to God – yet we know how God taught the lesson of substitution (and, more importantly, of His total abhorrence of human sacrifice, which was common during this period, during the time Israel was enslaved in Egypt and, later, during the time of the judges and kings). In the record in 2 Samuel of the closing years of King David's reign, we learn how David committed sin in his act of numbering the fighting men of Israel and, as a consequence, brought the Lord's judgement upon that nation. When confronted with God, he was commanded to make a burnt offering to Him. The site of the offering was the threshing floor of Araunah the Jebusite, and when David offered payment, this foreigner in essence said: 'You are the king, take the lot: animals and all for free.' David's answer was significant. He said: 'I will not make an offering to the LORD which has cost me nothing.' In the New Testament, we are told about 'the sacrifice of praise' (Hebrews 13:15). The best illustration in the New Testament is the record of Paul and Silas at Philippi. After experiencing sharp opposition to their preaching of Jesus Christ, the two were lashed and incarcerated in the innermost Roman dungeon. While others may have been questioning God's goodness, perhaps examining their lives for unconfessed sin, and calculating the length of time since their last tetanus boost, Paul and Silas were offering praise that was costing them dearly. We, in our pilgrimage into true worship, often have to overcome hurt and pain and hardship and loneliness and, perhaps, even doubts about God's goodness by commending God and praising Him for that goodness, love and mercy; His might and majesty; His righteous acts. As Paul and Silas entered into and reached the pinnacle of their worship, a mighty miracle took place. An earthquake opened the prison doors and shook off the heavy shackles.

What was the means that Jesus used to heal many who came to Him for healing? Many would have had tumours undetectable at that time in history. These tumours would have needed removal for complete and lasting healing to take place.

God heals in stages – Despite the claims of those Evangelicals who believe that the so-called 'sign gifts' that include healing were recalled during or soon after the apostolic era, healing as recorded in the Bible was not always instantaneous. In the Old Testament, the healing of Namaan the leper, which is referred to above (2 Kings 5), required seven dips in the Jordan before healing was accomplished. Instantaneous healing may well have occurred if Elisha had called 'on the name of the LORD his God, [and waved] his hand over the spot' as Namaan had expected (verse 11) or, at the very least, as the result of his first dip in the Jordan. Some writers have even suggested that Namaan's healing occurred as he immersed himself over the course of seven consecutive days, although there is no evidence of this from the text. Nor are we told if the leprous condition improved progressively each time Namaan immersed himself, or if the miracle took place on the seventh and final dip, a bit like the way the walls of Jericho crumbled on the seventh and final circuit of the Israelites on the seventh and final consecutive day. In the earthly ministry of Jesus, we find on one occasion a blind man being healed in stages so that he first saw 'men as trees' before the eventual full restoration of his sight took place (see Mark 8:24). The author's friend Paul Bennison, who has been previously mentioned, points out that for people who are deaf or blind, gradual healing is often more merciful to the sufferer, as the intensity of instantaneous previously or long unknown, light and sound invading the one being healed could be traumatic. Is this the reason why Jesus used this gradual approach with the blind man? If we do not read this as a deliberate act by Jesus, we are in danger of interpreting the event as showing a limitation of Jesus' power or a failure to 'get it right first time'. The Greek word *therapeo* is often used to describe the healings of Jesus and particularly those of the disciples. The word denotes the administration of a cure and is the root of our English words 'therapy' and 'therapeutic'. We would not expect to embark on a course of therapy and have an instant cure.

God heals through a creative act – God can create an organ or other part of the body that was not previously present. The introductory section of an extract from an internet article by Derek Thomas,[92] 'Creation Ex Nihilo', reads as follows:

> No sentence is more pregnant with meaning than the opening one of the Bible: 'In the beginning, God created the heavens and the earth' (Genesis 1:1). It tells us several things all at once, four of which are worth reflecting upon: First and foremost, it tells us that God is the ultimate Being. Before there was a universe, there was God. He exists independently of matter and sequence of time. God transcends space and time. He is not limited by spatial considerations (He is everywhere in His fullness continually). Nor is He locked into

---

92. Derek Thomas, 'Creation Ex Nihilo', Ligonier (1 January 2006), https://www.ligonier. org/learn/devotionals/creation-ex-nihilo (accessed 14 February 2022). Dr Derek Thomas is the Distinguished Visiting Professor of Systematic and Historical Theology at Reformed Theological Seminary in Jackson, Mississippi. He is also an associate minister at First Presbyterian Church in Columbia, South Carolina.

the present in any way. It is not strictly accurate to say that before the universe was created there was 'nothing,' for this, too, is a spatial and temporal idea: before the created universe existed, there was God. Theologians speak of God's immensity, infinity, and transcendence to describe this and our minds race at the thought of it, unable to take it in. All we can do is acquiesce and worship.

Second, everything that exists originates from God. Genesis employs a special Hebrew verb for the act of creation (bārā') the subject of which is always God. No other subject is employed or implied. Man, too, 'creates' (poetry, music, literature, architectural wonders, for example) but not in this sense. 'To create' is exclusively an act of God, and by employing it in the first and last verse of the creation story (1:1 and 2:4), the writer is employing something that looks like 'bookends' that encase the central idea that God is at work. Easy as this is to write (and read!), try to imagine the power it takes to bring into existence the entire cosmos!

Third, He creates 'out of nothing.' A grammatical possibility has given rise to at least one translation of the opening verses suggesting that when God began His work of creation, matter already existed: 'In the beginning when God created the heavens and the earth, the earth was a formless void' (NRSV). Contrast that with the English Standard Version: 'In the beginning, God created the heavens and the earth. The earth was without form and void.' The point of this second rendition is to emphasize a crucial issue that God created out of nothing (ex nihilo). Other ancient Near Eastern creation stories (from Egypt and Mesopotamia, for example) assume that their gods worked with material that already existed. However, biblical testimony here and elsewhere insists that at the point of the beginning there was nothing apart from God (Hebrews 11:3; Revelation 4:11), and what exists apart from God was brought into being by Him.

Fourth, and this is particularly interesting, that which He initially creates is not its final form. He creates in order to employ further artistry and design. Beginners in Hebrew at seminaries can often be heard repeating a phrase from Genesis 1:2: 'The earth was without form and void.' What God initially brought into being was 'tōhu vabōhu,' 'formless and empty mass.' Initially, the created universe had no distinctive shape; its structure would be formed by the artistry and design of God. In this sense, we are like God. We, too, fashion and mould and make things that are often beautiful. It is, in part, what Genesis 1:26–27 means by saying that Adam was created 'in the image of God.' Man, too, creates, or better, re-creates, shapes his environment in such a way as to reflect something pleasing and good. Once man fell, this capacity became as much a liability as a blessing: his capacity to fashion became a means to idolatry.

Back to the blind man of John 9:

> As he went along, he saw a man blind from birth.
> His disciples asked him, 'Rabbi, who sinned, this
> man or his parents, that he was born blind?'
> 'Neither this man nor his parents sinned,' said
> Jesus, 'but this happened so that the works of
> God might be displayed in him. As long as it is day,
> we must do the works of him who sent me. Night
> is coming, when no one can work. While I am in
> the world, I am the light of the world.' After saying
> this, he spat on the ground, made some mud with
> the saliva, and put it on the man's eyes. 'Go,' he
> told him, 'wash in the Pool of Siloam' (this word
> means 'Sent'). So the man went and washed, and
> came home seeing. (vv.1-7)

The author recalls the thinking of Teija Hoere, wife of Pastor
Hendrik Hoere of Cali, Colombia. She often reads this biblical
account and feels that it is obvious that this poor blind
man needed a pair of eyes. The Creator incarnate looked
to the ground and saw that the raw material[93] required for
the making of eyes was readily available, and so the 'dust
of the earth' infused with divine spittle was crafted into
eyeballs and placed into the man's empty sockets. This was
an entirely plausible interpretation of this story.

There is a great account of a creative healing miracle from
the life of Smith Wigglesworth. Under the subheading
'That You May Marvel,' we read:

---

93. 'Then the Lord God formed a man from the dust of the ground and breathed into his
nostrils the breath of life, and the man became a living being' (Genesis 2:7).

While staying in the home of a curate of the local Church of England [congregation], Wigglesworth and the curate were sitting together talking after supper. No doubt the subject of their conversation was that the poor fellow had no legs. Artificial limbs in those days were unlike the sophisticated limbs of today. Wigglesworth said to the man quite suddenly (which he often did when ministering in cases like this), 'Go and get a pair of new shoes in the morning.' The poor fellow thought it was some kind of joke. However, after Wigglesworth and the curate had retired to their respective rooms for the night, God said to the curate, 'Do as My servant hath said.' What a designation for any person – My servant! God was identifying Himself with Wigglesworth. There was no more sleep for the man that night. He rose up early, went down town, and stood waiting for the shoe shop to open. The manager eventually arrived and opened the shop for business. The curate went in and sat down. Presently an assistant came in and said, 'Good morning, sir. Can I help you?'

The man said, 'Yes, would you get me a pair of shoes, please.'

'Yes, sir. Size and colour?'

The curate hesitated. The assistant then saw his condition and said, 'Sorry, sir. We can't help you.'

'It's all right young man. But I do want a pair of shoes. Size 8 colour black.' The assistant went to get the requested shoes. A few minutes later he returned and handed them to the man. The man put one stump into a shoe and *instantly a foot and leg formed!* Then *the same thing happened with the other leg!* He walked out of that shop not only with a new pair of shoes, but also with a new pair of legs!! Wigglesworth was not surprised. He had expected the result. He often made remarks like this, 'As far as God is concerned, there is no difference between forming a limb and healing a broken bone.'[94]

God heals by removing the diabolical cause of the illness – We have discussed at length in the previous section how it is possible for spirits of infirmity to invade the human body to varying degrees, producing symptoms consistent with organic diseases. The removal of the offending spirits will produce healing in the individual, including the removal of the associated symptoms, as in the case of the crippled woman healed by Jesus on the Sabbath (Luke 13:12-13).

Just as God chooses to reveal Himself as the God of order, He also demonstrates how He is a God who is responsive. As far as humankind is concerned, because He is Love, God responds to need. Our need of a Saviour brought about the incarnation, the sinless life and the atoning death of the Lord Jesus Christ. He was able to state of Himself:

> The Spirit of the Lord is on me, because he has anointed me to preach good news to the poor. He has sent me to proclaim freedom for the prisoners and recovery of sight for the blind, to set the oppressed free, to proclaim the year of the Lord's favour. (Luke 4:18-19)

94. Hibbert, Albert, *Smith Wigglesworth: The Secret of His Power* (Shippensburg, PA: Destiny Image, 1987), p.17; emphasis added.

However, even in our needy state, His method of being responsive is by humankind exercising, at some level, faith in Him – choosing to believe what He says about Himself and us, and then acting on the basis of that belief. In the arena of healing, it seems that there are four levels of faith that the Healer responds to. Firstly, there is individual or personal faith. Secondly, there is vicarious faith, where the sick person is an unbeliever or is too sick or disturbed to exercise personal faith, and by which a healing gift operates. Thirdly, there is united faith, as in the prayer of agreement or where intercession is being made on behalf of a sick person in accordance with James 5. Fourthly, there is community faith, expressed in the negative by Jesus, for example, when He marvelled at the lack of community faith in His hometown of Nazareth (Mark 6:5). This lack of community faith prevented Him from performing mighty miracles, so we can conclude conversely that an abundance of such faith would have provided, and does provide, the conditions for the miraculous to take place.

The need for, and the exercising of, faith is covered in a later section of this work.

The Healing Ministry of Jesus

In general, there are three lines of belief that we can embrace in relation to Christ's purpose in performing the miracles that are recorded by the four evangelists. The first line of belief is that He performed them to demonstrate His sovereignty, as God, as revealed in the Second Person of the Trinity. This is very clearly the theme of John's gospel – he chooses several of Jesus' miracles, including notable healings, and records them in his gospel as 'signs'.

The changing of water into wine at the wedding in Cana, near Jesus' home town, is referred to by John as the first of these *signs*. He states, 'And his disciples believed on him.' It seems that John intended to conclude his gospel at the end of chapter 20[95] because, there, he summarises his narrative. He states that, although Jesus did many other miracles, he selected the ones he recorded so that the reader would believe that Jesus is the Son of God and, by believing, would have eternal life.

The second line of belief is that He performed them to demonstrate the qualities of a coming Kingdom that He would inaugurate. In that Kingdom there would be no want of food or drink, no sickness or disease, no pain or death, no destructive forces of nature, and that all of His miracles serve to illustrate this.

The third line of belief is that He performed them not because He was God but because He was a man anointed of the Holy Spirit. This is very much the emphasis of Luke, and we have already previously used his quotation from Acts when he describes Jesus in this way. This line of belief is not intended to diminish the divinity of Christ in any way, but rather to emphasise His deliberate emptying of Himself[96] of His divine attributes to depend on the revelation and power of the Holy Spirit. Bickersteck recognises this thinking as being orthodox in his work on the Trinity saying:

> We have seen that no exception can be taken against his Almighty power as God from the

---

95. John produced his final 'sequel' chapter seemingly to quash the popular rumour among the early believers that he, John, would not die before Christ's return.
96. Philippians 2.

words 'I can of mine own self do nothing' because as man, he wrought his miracles, not by virtue of his deity, which was ever inherent in him, but by virtue of a perfect faith in the power of the Father, through the plenitude of the Holy Ghost. Though as God ever and always to do all things, he, of his own Divine will, resolved not to exert his personal omnipotence betwixt his incarnation and his crucifixion. This resolution was part of the emptying spoken of, Phil. ii. 7.[97]

The first line of thinking noted above is very much the emphasis of Reformed theology, which majors on the sovereignty of God, particularly in the doctrine of election. It is very easy to see how John's gospel supports this line of belief; however, it is John who, in the context of Jesus' miracles, records Jesus as having said to His disciples: 'Whoever believes in me will do the works I have been doing, and they will do even greater things than these because I am going to the Father' (John 14:12). *Clearly John is not saying that followers of Jesus who are performing the miracles are also manifesting divinity!* In fact, much earlier in human history Moses, Elijah and Elisha performed miracles that were of similar calibre to those performed by Jesus during His earthly ministry: the cleansing of the leprous as in the account of Namaan (2 Kings 5); the multiplication of organic material as with the widow's oil (1 Kings 17); power over the weather, in the case of Elijah's prophecy that there would be no rain in Israel (1 Kings 18); power over the laws of nature and physics as in the parting of the Red Sea (Exodus 13) and the floating

---

97. Bickersteth, Edward Henry, *The Trinity* (Grand Rapids, MI: Kregal Publications, 1957), p.99.

axe-head (2 Kings 6); the raising of the dead (2 Kings 4) . . . and so the list continues. *Moses, Elijah and Elisha were not demonstrating divinity!*

Getting below the surface of some of the signs recorded by John is a worthwhile exercise, since, as we will see, it was the *outcomes* of the miraculous healings performed by Jesus, rather than the healings themselves, that demonstrated His divinity. In John 5 we find the record of an invalid being healed at the Pool of Bethesda. This was an outstanding miracle, but its ultimate motive was for Jesus to proclaim to the religious leaders that in His divinity, He was permitted to work on the Sabbath – no apostle or follower of Jesus has ever been, or ever will be afforded that right. This theme is backed up by Matthew and Luke in their gospels, where Jesus is presented as 'Lord of the Sabbath'. In John 9, the result of the healing of the blind man was that he *worshipped Jesus*. No apostle or follower of Jesus has or ever will be afforded the right to be worshipped. When Jesus healed the paralytic at Peter's house, as recorded in the first chapter of Mark's gospel, He first pronounced that the man's sins had been forgiven. The religious leaders correctly concluded among themselves that only God could forgive sin, but incorrectly concluded that Jesus was simply a man. When Peter and John healed the crippled man at the Beautiful Gate of the Temple, as recorded in Acts 3, they performed a similar miracle to those performed by Jesus at Peter's house and by the Pool of Bethesda; however, they did not assume to forgive the man's sins – only God could do that.

The second line of thinking noted above is a valid expression of Jesus' earthly ministry. Jesus certainly heralded a new era. John the Baptist came preaching: 'Repent, for the kingdom of heaven has come near' (Matthew 3:2), and after John was put in prison, Jesus proclaimed, 'The kingdom of God has come near' (Mark 1:15b). The Jewish people expected a messiah who would restore the kingdom of David in an era of peace and prosperity, with military supremacy and freedom from their enemies. The Kingdom principles that Jesus demonstrated throughout His earthly ministry turned many of the Jewish ideals on their head! Moreover, Jesus' healings were borne primarily out of compassion for the sufferers rather than to make a statement of any kind. Henry Chadwick, the notable church historian, states:

> He performs cures of both body and mind but from compassion, not to impress doubters. People who demanded miracles to prove his divine mission were refused.[98]

The third line of thinking regarding Jesus' earthly ministry is supported by Peter, as recorded by Luke:

> Then Peter began to speak: 'I now realise how true it is that God does not show favouritism but accepts from every nation the one who fears him and does what is right. You know the message God sent to the people of Israel, announcing the good news of peace through Jesus Christ, who is Lord of all. You know what has happened throughout the province of Judea, beginning in Galilee after the baptism that John preached – how *God*

98. McManners, John, ed., *The Oxford Illustrated History of Christianity* (Oxford: Oxford University Press, 1992), cites Chadwick, p.21.

anointed Jesus of Nazareth with the Holy Spirit and power, and how he went around doing good and healing all who were under the power of the devil, because God was with him. (Acts 10:34-38, emphasis added)

But before Peter had ever met Him, Jesus had lived for thirty years without there being any evidence of a supernatural ministry. We have a brief insight into His wisdom when, at the age of twelve, He was found amazing those in the Temple with His insights (Luke 2:41-50). But family life in the home of Joseph of Nazareth, the carpenter, must have been normal enough such that 'even his own brothers did not believe in him' (John 7:5). It was only when He was baptised by John in the River Jordan, and when the Holy Spirit descended on Him and remained (John 1:32), that He embarked on His teaching and miracle ministry.

We can, however, imagine His prayer life reflecting an unbroken communion with His Father during all His earthly years but, for His first thirty years on earth, He had, in some sense, been bereft of the Third Person of the Trinity, otherwise this baptismal anointing would not have been required. This concept is consistent with Paul's description of Christ's servanthood in his letter to the Philippians: 'Who, being in very nature God, did not consider equality with God something to be used to his own advantage; rather he made himself nothing' (2:6-7a).

Jesus of Nazareth had spent thirty years thirsting for the Holy Spirit!

And so, He may well have identified with the psalmist when he said:

As the deer pants for streams of water, so my soul pants for you, my God. My soul thirsts for God, for the living God. When can I go and meet with God? (Psalm 42:1-2)

And:

You, God, are my God, earnestly I seek you; I thirst for you, my whole being longs for you, in a dry and parched land where there is no water. (Psalm 63:1)

It was no wonder He was able to say to a thirsty woman at the side of Jacob's well in Sychar:

'Everyone who drinks this water will be thirsty again, but whoever drinks the water I give them will never thirst. Indeed, the water I give them will become in them a spring of water welling up to eternal life.' The woman said to him, 'Sir, give me this water so that I won't get thirsty and have to keep coming here to draw water.' (John 4:13-15)

He had known that thirst Himself! When He spoke at the Feast in Jerusalem on the last and greatest day, he said in a loud voice:

'Let anyone who is thirsty come to me and drink.[99] Whoever believes in me, as Scripture has said, rivers of living water will flow from within them.' By this he meant the Spirit, whom those who believed in him were later to receive. Up to that

---

99.   See Isaiah 55:1: 'Come, all you who are thirsty, come to the waters; and you who have no money, come, buy and eat! Come, buy wine and milk without money and without cost.'

time the Spirit had not been given, since Jesus had not yet been glorified. (John 7:37-39)

He was speaking from the heart! But He was to know that thirsting again, like His forebear, when he was in exile and the Philistine garrison was at Bethlehem. At that time, David longed for water and said:

'Oh, that someone would get me a drink of water from the well near the gate of Bethlehem!' So the three mighty warriors broke through the Philistine lines, drew water from the well near the gate of Bethlehem and carried it back to David. But he refused to drink it; instead, he poured it out before the LORD. (2 Samuel 23:15b-16)

But His thirsting was on an infinitely greater scale:

So the soldiers took charge of Jesus. Carrying his own cross, he went out to the place of the Skull (which in Aramaic is called Golgotha). There they crucified him . . . Jesus said, 'I am thirsty.' (John 19:16b-18, 28)

It is inconceivable that John the evangelist, who had used the term 'thirsty' only twice before in his gospel, and only with reference to the Holy Spirit, could not have seen the significance of Jesus' words on the cross. We often hear of how God the Father, who could not look on sin, turned away from God the Son as He was crucified, 'made to be sin for us, who knew no sin' (2 Corinthians 5:21 KJV).

Jesus of Nazareth had spent thirty years thirsting for the Holy Spirit! When He hung on the cross, He was forsaken not only by God the Father but also by God the Holy Spirit!

And so, He cried out, 'I am thirsty!' Just as the sign of Jesus of Nazareth's acceptance by His Father was the anointing of the Holy Spirit at the time of His baptism, so the sign of His being forsaken by that same Father was the withdrawal of that same Holy Spirit.

And so, this concept of a Man anointed of the Holy Spirit gives us a pioneering example to follow. In the context of miraculous works, however, He indicates how we can expect to exceed His accomplishments!

> Believe me when I say that I am in the Father and the Father is in me; *or at least believe on the evidence of the works* themselves. Very truly I tell you, *whoever believes in me will do the works I have been doing, and they will do even greater things than these,*[100] *because I am going to the Father.* And I will do whatever you ask in my name, so that the Father may be glorified in the Son. You may ask me for anything in my name, and I will do it. If you love me, keep my commands. And I will ask the Father, and he will give you another advocate to help you and be with you for ever – the Spirit of truth. (John 14:11-17, emphasis added)

---

100. Presumably, one reason that this standard is achievable is because most Christian believers will have longer than three years to minister under the anointing of the Holy Spirit. Jesus' public earthly ministry was brief and therefore had temporal and geographical limitations. When this same writer, John, is drawing his gospel to a conclusion, he writes: 'Jesus performed many other signs in the presence of his disciples, which are not recorded in this book' (20:30). In the epilogue chapter that follows, he concludes: 'Jesus did many other things as well. If every one of them were written down, I suppose that even the whole world would not have room for the books that would be written' (21:25). John is neither exaggerating nor putting an unlimited label on Jesus' earthly ministry, but recalling how, in his prologue, he credits Jesus as the eternal Logos and as the One without whom 'nothing was made that has been made' (1:3b).

This proclamation is clearly meant not only for the disciples immediately present, but also for 'whoever believes' in Jesus. The latter portion of the passage gives us the key as to how this accomplishment can be achieved – the giving of the Spirit of truth to the Christian. This happened at the festival of Pentecost seven weeks after Jesus' death. It is by that Holy Spirit that we have been bestowed power and gifting. One of the specific supernatural gifts of the Holy Spirit is the gift of healing.

The Spiritual Gift of Healing

The gifts listed in 1 Corinthians 12 are sometimes categorised under the headings 'miraculous' and 'non-miraculous'. Gifts of healing belong to the miraculous category, together with working of miracles, prophecy, discernment of spirits, tongues and interpretation of tongues (v.10). For the purpose of the subject we are studying, those who deny that those gifts of the Spirit classified above as 'miraculous' are not in operation in the Church at present because they have ceased to operate, are referred to as Cessationists. There follows a crude summary of the system of theological belief leading one to take a Cessationist position and why the author does not accept the Cessationist premise.

Firstly, there is the belief that only the original apostles had the ability to work miracles conferred upon them. An outspoken critic of the continuance of the miraculous gifts states: 'The disciples are nowhere portrayed as granting others the power they enjoyed.'[101] Yet according to Mark 16:16-18, it was those who believed in the message of the

---

101. Gross, p.43.

apostles' preaching who 'shall lay hands on the sick, and they shall recover' (KJV). How was power conferred that would accomplish this? It is also made clear by Mark that only the eleven were present at this commissioning. How then do we assume Judas' replacement, Matthias (Acts 1:26), received his apostolic gifting? More notable is the account in Acts 9 of the mysterious Ananias of Damascus. He is not even mentioned outside of this incident let alone described as an apostle, and yet he was supernaturally guided to Saul of Tarsus and placed his hands upon him not only to administer a miraculous healing in the restoring of Saul's sight, but also to confer upon him an in-filling of the Holy Spirit (9:17). Equally mysterious is the 'someone' of Mark 9:38-40: '"Teacher," said John, "we saw someone driving out demons in your name and we told him to stop, because he was not one of us." "Do not stop him," Jesus said. "For no one who does a miracle in my name can in the next moment say anything bad about me, for whoever is not against us is for us."' Obviously, this person had a supernatural gift that enabled him to cast out demons. Not only was he not an apostle, he wasn't even known to the apostles!

Secondly, there is a belief that the spiritual gift of prophecy became redundant when the New Testament canon was fixed; if one supernatural or 'sign' gift (demonstrating credence to the bearer of the gift as an apostle) was redundant, then others may also be in that same category, namely all of the so-called miraculous sign gifts. Nevertheless, Paul, within this New Testament canon of Scripture, exhorts us *not* to despise prophesies and *not* to forbid speaking in tongues, another of the so-called sign gifts.

Thirdly, while the early Pentecostals taught that a medicinal crutch is tantamount to an absence of faith (and this is presently taught by some), others claimed that medical and surgical means were positively evil and that doctors, and medical people in general, were servants of the devil.[102] This view appears to contradict Paul's exhortation to Timothy to use a little wine for medicinal purposes, and now seems to have disappeared from mainstream classical Pentecostal teaching for practical reasons.

Fourthly, many theologians deny that a post-conversion baptism of the Holy Spirit is a valid Christian experience outside of the apostolic era. 'It is commonly believed among Pentecostals and Neo-Pentecostals that the Christian is not endowed with his particular gift or gifts [healing or healings] of the Spirit until he or she is baptised with, or in, the Holy Spirit.'[103] Because this post-conversion baptism is emphasised by Pentecostals as the event during which Spiritual gifts are conferred, the 'baby' of supernatural gifts has been thrown out with the 'bathwater' of post-conversion Spirit baptism. Many neo-Pentecostals who worship within mainstream denominations accept and promote the survival of the supernatural gifts, which includes healing, without the express baptism in the Spirit of the individual, preferring to emphasise 'the importance of an ongoing practical experience of being filled with the Spirit'.[104]

---

102. Manwaring, Paul, *Kisses From a Good God* (Shippensburg, PA: Destiny Image, 2012), p.99. By contrast, Paul Manwaring of Bethel Church in Redding, California, states: 'We need to be careful that we do not view our doctors and healthcare workers as agents of the devil – our enemy and source of disease – although they are required to speak of what may appear negative. Doctors are trained to deliver a diagnosis, which is distinctly different from speaking a curse.'
103. Unger, Merrill F., *The Baptism and Gifts of the Holy Spirit* (Chicago, IL: Moody, 1974), p.133.
104. Lane, p.255.

Fifthly, the alleged actions and lifestyles of some who claim to have received these miraculous gifts have brought the gifts themselves into disrepute. J.G.S.S. Thomson and W.A. Ellwell write, 'Gifts of healing are permanent gifts of the Spirit to the church but are properly exercised only by men of the Spirit, and of humility and faith.'[105]

Sixthly, as noted in the introduction and several times in earlier sections of this work, there is the observation that the present day 'miraculous healing' ministry is distinctly lacking in calibre and volume, compared with healing ministry described in the gospels and in the book of Acts. This gives reinforcement to the statement of Warrington quoted earlier: 'The dissimilarity in success rates between Christians then and today is significant and inexplicable if both groups received the same command.'[106] As previously argued, however, allegations that biblical healings were always instantaneous and permanent are not well founded. Jesus Himself healed in stages in the restoration of sight. One afflicted person 'began to recover' at the very hour that Jesus spoke a healing word and sadly, although perfectly restored from the illness that first claimed his life, poor Lazarus had to die once again as a result of some fatal cause, which we would like to believe was old age. It is appropriate also to state here, as elsewhere, that Jesus could do no mighty miracles in Nazareth because of the people's unbelief. Observations and reports of happenings in countries further afield, where Christian revival is in operation, may provide better examples of miraculous healings that are of authentic apostolic standard.[107]

---

105. Elwell, p.1043.
106. Warrington, p.150.
107. However, see footnote #17.

Lastly, the past lack of systematic theologians from the Pentecostal and Charismatic camps has left the case for the continuance of the gifts relying, in many cases, on what are seen to be experiential claims, rather than biblical premises. This situation has now begun to change.

One of the main arguments used by Cessationists, based on the content of 1 Corinthians 13, is that 'tongues will cease, prophecies will cease'; namely sign gifts will cease when that which is perfect appears. They interpret this perfection to have now appeared in the content of the canon of New Testament Scriptures. With regard to this interpretation, Baptist minister Herbert Carson states:

> It has only been the desperate need to try and buttress an argument against the continuance of the charismata that has led to the current popularity in some circles of an interpretation that really is quite a novelty, and a rather fanciful novelty at that, in the history of expounding the Scriptures.[108]

The fact that it was the late 2nd century before this New Testament canon of Scripture was fixed shows that subsequent generations from the time of the first apostles must have retained the 'sign gifts' for their authentication, if that indeed was the purpose of the gifts. Additionally, the content of the passages of 1 Corinthians 12 must have been considered to be relevant contemporary pastoral issues for the book to be considered canonical. For those who dispute the authenticity of the latter portion of Mark 16, which links the gifts of healing and speaking in tongues with the Great Commission, it is noteworthy that if these verses are later additions, that only serves to show that the

---

108. Carson, p.50.

sign gifts referred to were still accompanying those who had believed at that later time.

Writings by the Church Fathers (Irenaeus, Origen, Justin Martyr, Tertullian and Augustine[109]) and afterwards, indicate that the miraculous gifts continued to be exercised in the post-apostolic and post-canonical periods. Those who do not support the continued operation of the gifts cite these writings as illustrating that God did and does intervene miraculously in the area of healing from time to time, but that much of Church history is devoid of such miracles. Many from this school of belief are Reformed theology scholars who suspect much superstition and exaggeration existed in the writings of the Roman Church. Yet we read about the beliefs and practices supporting the continuance of the healing gift in the post-Reformation era. Luther himself is credited with the gift of healing, particularly as evidenced in the narrative relating to the raising up of his friend Melanthon from his deathbed to enjoy continuing good health. The influential Moravian, Count Nicholas von Zinzendorf (1700-1760), witnessed:

> We have had undeniable proofs . . . in the healing of maladies in themselves incurable, such as cancers, consumptions, when the patient was in the agonies of death, etc. all by means of prayer, or of a single word.[110]

John Wesley records how his theology with regard to the miraculous was formed on one occasion through the reading of a book. He wrote on 15 August 1750:

---

109. Elwell, p.498. Wimber includes in an appendix to the book *Power Evangelism: Signs and Wonders Today* (London: Hodder & Stoughton, 1985) writings from each of the Church Fathers in support of the continuance of the gifts.
110. Woolmer, p. 181, quoting A.J. Gordon, *The Three Great Classics on Divine Healing*.

> I was fully convinced of what I had once suspected: (1) That the Montanists . . . were real, scriptural Christians; and (2) The grand reason why the miraculous gifts were so soon withdrawn, was not only that faith and holiness were well nigh lost, but that dry, formal, orthodox men began even then to ridicule whatever gift they had not themselves, and to decry them all as either madness or imposture.[111]

Dickinson states that: 'John Wesley was not consistent with his view that miracles ceased when the [Roman] Empire became Christian.'[112] In a letter to Thomas Church in June 1746, Wesley wrote:

> I do not recollect any scripture wherein we are taught that miracles were to be confined within the limits either of the apostolic or the Cyprianic age, or of any period of time, longer or shorter, even till the restitution of all things.[113]

However, in fairness to Wesley, he may not be stating that God deliberately withdrew the gifts, *but rather that the Holy Spirit withdrew, or was quenched, as a response to man's dry orthodoxy*. One possible contributory factor to this lack of the use of miraculous gifts, including healing, was the reaction of Church orthodoxy, in the 2nd century, to the Montanist movement[114] to which Wesley refers.

---

111. Wimber, *Power Evangelism*, p.165. Wimber quotes Wesley's journal.
112. Dickinson, Robert, *God Does Heal Today* (Carlisle: Paternoster, 1995), p.138.
113. Wimber, *Power Evangelism*, p.165. Wimber quotes Wesley's letter.
114. The Montanists were 2nd-century Christian followers of a self-claimed prophet, Montanus, who, together with his female assistants, proclaimed prophetic utterances, often in trances and through unknown tongues, many relating to the near return of Christ. Although supported to an extent by Tertullian, the movement was pronounced as being heretical by the orthodox leaders, and its leaders and followers formally excommunicated. The Montanists will be considered further, later in this work.

This may have had the effect of quenching the miraculous working of the Holy Spirit for many centuries through a prejudiced rather than a cautious approach to embracing any practices or manifestations that appeared to be out of the ordinary.[115] We shall return to this theme at a later stage.

The operation of miraculous gifts, including healing gifts is, according to Peter, a characteristic of the last days. The expression 'last days' used by Peter and recorded by Luke in Acts 2 is a quotation from Joel's prophecy as recorded in the Septuagint.[116] This particular expression is used in two other passages in the New Testament. In his letter to Timothy, Paul explains that in the 'last days' perilous times will come, and in Hebrews the writer states that in the past God spoke through the prophets but in these 'last days' He has spoken through His Son. There is no room for any dispensational parenthesis. Simply put, this expression as used in the New Testament, teaches that the 'last days' that began at Pentecost, have continued until the present and will continue until the time of Christ's return.

Paul is clear that all of the gifts he discusses are for the building-up of the Church and are given by the Spirit as the Spirit determines. To exclude the miraculous gifts during any period of the Church's existence is to ignore Paul's warning about the all-inclusiveness that is to be applied to the parts of the 'body', which is the immediate scriptural context of the Corinthian passage. Yet Martin's commentary on 1 Corinthians 12 states:

> The danger in refusing this distinction [between gifts of permanent validity and gifts of temporary

---

115. This prejudice is obvious in our own age.
116. See footnote #80.

and apostolic usage, now withdrawn] is seen in attempts to recapture 'apostolic Christianity' . . . we are guilty of theological anachronism, harking back to a past which is beyond recall.[117]

An unfortunate danger of the Cessationist line of thought is that it could be used in a similar way to argue that the need for the preaching of the gospel (in the evangelistic sense) has also passed:[118]

- Only the original apostles were personally commissioned by Jesus for this preaching work;
- The existence of the canon of New Testament Scriptures means that people can read its content or have it read to them and respond without the need for preaching.

In concluding this section, we must recognise that the purpose of Paul's instructions in the 1 Corinthians 12 passage is to stress the proper use of the gifts within the Church and to demonstrate that they exist for the common good. The more spectacular gifts need a greater degree of order to prevent their indiscriminate use, and there is a danger of emphasising one gift over another. According to J.G.S.S. Thomson and W.A. Elwell, this has 'led inevitably to the institutional ecclesiasticism and the inevitable corresponding loss of the church's awareness of the Spirit's presence and the experience of the Spirit's power'.[119] If healing gifts have been distributed to individuals in a contemporary local church setting, the church must permit

---

117. Martin, Ralph P., *1 and 2 Corinthians and Galatians* (London: Scripture Union, 1968), pp.32-33.
118. This was an error that was actually embraced by Calvin and the early Reformers in their taking the doctrine of predestination to its extreme.
119. Elwell, p.1046.

those gifts to be practised. If these gifts are in operation, then we should expect them to produce the same results as they produced for the apostles.

Healing Prayer

For those who reject the continuance of supernatural gifts such as healing, but hold to the prospect of divine healing, as any orthodox Christian must, James 5:14-16 gives us a model for intercessory healing prayer. It is evident that intercessory prayer is being contemplated since the 'prayer of faith' refers to the prayers of the elders rather than the prayer of the sick person.[120]

These verses have been interpreted in various ways by commentators and theologians. Some believe they seem to provide the alternative as to how divine healing should operate in this age, and are cited as thus by many; nevertheless, the association of what is seen as a symbolic application of the oil with the anointing of the Holy Spirit has left most non-Charismatic and non-Pentecostal churches uncomfortable with the practice as described.

Dr Peter Masters states that 'James 5 excludes such activities as the dispensing or calling down of the Holy Spirit',[121] and has said that the anointing with oil has a practical rather than a spiritual meaning as the 'standard medical remedy', since the Greek word *aleipho* is associated with the application of a medical rub rather than a

---

120. This is especially noteworthy in the context of where it is claimed by Charismatics and Pentecostals that some individuals are not healed on account of their lack of faith, thus shifting the responsibility away from the one administering the healing either through the gift of healing or by prayer. This passage places a distinct onus upon the 'healer'.
121. Masters, pp.139-140.

ceremonial anointing, which would have been represented by the word *chrio*.[122] He chooses, however, to ignore that the same Greek word that is used in James 5 is also used by the evangelist in Mark 6:13 to record the activities of the disciples when they were engaging in their supernatural healing and deliverance ministry. Nor does he explain why this service of anointing should be linked closely with the words 'In the name of the Lord', which appears to signify that a more ceremonial event is being implied. Others see a very limited application of James 5. Theodore Epp states: 'The reason for calling the elders was apparently because the sickness referred to by James was a sickness which resulted from sin.'[123] He cites 1 Corinthians 11:29-30, which states that some at the church in Corinth had become weak and sickly as a result of their sin of dishonouring God at the Lord's Supper; some had even died. He ignores, however, the little word '*If* they have sinned . . .' in the James 5 text. Others see the book as an exclusively Jewish treatise[124] 'to the twelve tribes scattered abroad', with a particular relevance to the Old Covenant, where freedom from disease is associated with obedience to the covenant. However, these were Jewish Christians, as were many of the Early Church, who were, at that time, living under the New Covenant. This selective adherence to the instruction of the New Testament canon is dangerous and self-defeating.

If we are to regard the instructions of James 5 as an instruction in how to heal the sick in the absence of the

---

122. Masters, p.147.
123. Epp, Theodore H., James: *The Epistle of Applied Christianity* (Lincoln, NE: Back to the Bible, 1980), p.247.
124. See Gaebelein, p.80.

continuance of the New Testament gift of healing we are still faced with a dilemma. *James appears to lead us to expect a 100 per cent success rate, and against this measure we, as the Church of the day, are still failing miserably.*

Christian Healing Practices

o———<o>———o

What we believe dictates what we practise – what we believe about Jesus and His purposes in doing miracles; what we believe about the continuance of the supernatural gifts of the Spirit in the post-Apostolic era.

Services for Healing

For those who do not emphasise the prospect of divine healing and do not regard the gift of healing to be in operation in today's Church age, much of Church life will be bereft of healing prayer, the laying on of hands or anointing with oil in the name of Jesus Christ. Increasingly, nevertheless, Christian churches from many different denominations are offering healing prayer, often advertised as 'healing prayer and the laying on of hands'.[125] Typically, the service will include a time of praise and worship, using music, followed by a short sermon associated with the healing ministry to stimulate faith and encourage individuals to participate in receiving the prayer ministry. The service will then move into healing prayer, with each participant being prayed with by pairs of individuals from a specially trained prayer ministry team. During

---

125. This is the model adopted by Interdenominational Divine Healing Ministries – see footnote #2 above.

this prayer time, those praying will place their hands on those receiving prayer, often on the place where pain is being experienced or close to the position of a diseased organ in the body, where this is practical. On occasion, anointing the forehead of the individual with oil[126] will accompany the prayers. In a more formal Anglican setting, the ministry can be conducted liturgically using, for example, a shortened form of 'Series Two' evensong, including a canticle such as 'Salvator Mundi', which contains many biblical truths pertinent to Christian healing. Again, after the sermon, recipients are invited to come forward to the communion rail, where prayer is administered together with the laying on of hands.[127] Services of this type allow for a wide spectrum of theological convictions on the subject of healing on the part of those who minister healing, the recipients of the ministry and the worshipping congregation. In some cases, prayer by proxy is practised. When this takes place, a representative of the sick person (who, perhaps, because of the seriousness of the ailment, or because of geographical distance or hospitalisation, cannot be present), often a close relative, friend or spouse, is prayed with on the person's behalf together with the laying on of hands. Some churches regard this practice as unbiblical and rather choose to place their hands upon, and pray over a handkerchief, which is then taken and placed on the sick person, with Acts 19:12 being cited in support. In any case, where contact is made directly, with or without oil, or through an object, a gift of the Holy Spirit is generally believed to be in operation.

---

126. Sometimes referred to as the 'oil of gladness', based on Isaiah 60.
127. Lawrence, p.18.

Public Prayer and/or Declaration

A second approach which is used in mainstream denominations, Pentecostal churches and independent Evangelical assemblies, is where a public prayer is led from the 'front', with individuals' names read out, perhaps with a brief description of their condition. This gives an opportunity for the entire congregation to agree in prayer together in a focused way. Thus, this event is a topical prayer meeting, with more emphasis on God's willingness to hear and answer prayer according to His will, in much the same way as He would about any other subject that concerns His children. For this reason, there is less emphasis on the miraculous in general, and often no emphasis whatsoever on the supernatural gift of healing administered by the laying on of hands. Such expressions as 'Guide the hands of the surgeon',[128] 'Help them [the individual being prayed for] respond to treatment' and 'Comfort them at this difficult time' are commonplace in this kind of healing ministry.

A Pentecostal Approach

Also available is the Pentecostal approach to divine healing where, like the second approach above, a notable factor is corporate participation, but with a distinct emphasis on the miraculous and the supernatural. It will usually be conducted as part of a congregational meeting within the local church setting. The purpose of this is to maximise faith in Christ,[129]

---

128. Johnson, Bill, *When Heaven Invades Earth* (Shippensburg, PA: Destiny Image, 2003), pp.17-18. Foreword by Jack Taylor.
129. Wimber, *Power Evangelism*, p.95. Wimber tells of the church that did not believe that God still heals today. A man whose wife was so ill that the doctors did not expect her to make it through the night called the elders to pray and anoint her with oil. The next day, to their surprise, she walked out of the hospital. The doctors called it a miracle. Wimber says: 'What is remarkable is that the elders never told the congregation what happened', thus congregational faith was not heightened and encouraged.

not only for healing but also for salvation in response to miraculous healings, a phenomenon Wimber[130] refers to as 'Power Evangelism', as in the title of his book. At the time of writing this section, the Toronto Airport Christian Fellowship Church is enjoying a quarter of a century of a local revival that has had international repercussions. The movement that has been termed the 'Toronto Blessing' has experienced supernatural healing and deliverance regularly at its meetings down through the years, under former joint pastors John and Carol Arnott and their successors. A prominent feature of these worship services is that when an attendee's healing occurs spontaneously during the worship time or as a result of prayer, it is not unusual for an altar call to immediately follow and for dozens of people to make a Christian commitment as a response to the healing or indeed multiple healings that have just taken place.

In the Pentecostal practice of Christian healing, there is a great emphasis on the need for the would-be recipient of healing to claim his or her healing. And so, faith must play an important part. One other prominent feature in this type of service, demonstrating its Pentecostal and Charismatic origins, is the use of 'words of knowledge'. Through this spiritual gift, a revelation is given to the leader or pastor with regard to the ailments that are going to be healed, or

---

130. John Wimber's own interest in miraculous healing was stimulated as he studied church growth. Signs and wonders accompanied the phenomenal growth of the Full Gospel Central Church in Seoul, South Korea, pastored by Paul Yonggi Cho. Wimber later promoted this style of healing as part of his own ministry. It is often recorded that where there is significant church growth or local revival, signs and wonders, including miraculous healings together with personal deliverances, are always present. There is doubtless an element of trying to create a revival situation by introducing these ministries at a local church level without recognising that they may be the results and outworking of revival rather than the recipe or conditions for revival. The connection between spiritual revival and miraculous signs and wonders, including healing, are discussed in a later section of this work.

to otherwise identify persons who are to be ministered to on that occasion. This is usually before the healing takes place. It is obvious that those who reject the spiritual gift of healing, regarding it to have ceased to operate from the time of the apostles, will equally reject the alleged use of this gift of knowledge.

James 5

A fourth and final[131] approach to Christian healing is the previously mentioned practice of James 5:14ff:

> Is any sick among you? Let him call for the elders of the church; and let them pray over him, anointing him with oil in the name of the Lord: And the prayer of faith shall save the sick, and the Lord shall raise him up. (KJV)

This is the practice advocated by Evangelicals who believe that the spiritual gift of healing is no longer in use. However, as noted above, it is rarely practised as prescribed. The original setting appears to have been the home of the sick person rather than at a public meeting.

All of the practices summarised above are claimed by their respective advocates to be strictly biblical, and we have noted the scriptural premise upon which each is based. Yet the author's experience is that despite the successes cited, there are many more failures. Most honest readers will admit the same. Since there is a significant emphasis

---

131. 'Final' only in the sense of this present work. There may be other variations on the themes of the four practices noted and possibly a fifth where healing is practised as an integral part of the celebration of the sacrament of the Lord's Supper. See footnote #30 for the full extent of the connection.

placed on faith in all of the various practices of Christian healing, and we have previously noted the importance of faith at various levels, then we may be drawn to conclude that failure in Christian healing is the result of lack of faith. This premise is discussed later in this work.

Factors That Hinder Success

The above arguments from Scripture direct us to consider the following premises:

a) That sickness is of the devil, whose work Jesus Christ came to destroy through His life, death and resurrection;

b) That certain provisions have been made, particularly through Christ's passion, whereby healing from sickness can be appropriated and enjoyed;

c) That gifts of healing are in operation in this age, as distributed by the Holy Spirit in accordance with the divine will;

d) That where these gifts of healing are not in operation in a local church setting, for whatever reason, healing can be administered by prayer and anointing with oil; and

e) That, as a result of these provisions, the universal Church should be experiencing a high level of success in its ministry of healing.

This is a summary of the author's personal convictions. It is also the author's experience that the universal Church in general and the local churches of the Western world in particular are not presently enjoying this high level of success, even where their articles of faith and congregational practices are consistent with the aforementioned premises. The various sections in this chapter therefore address the possible reasons for the present low levels of success. In his analysis of the ministry of Smith Wigglesworth, Peter J. Madden touches on having the need to offer similar explanations when he comments:

> He read how the Lord worked through the apostles in the Book of Acts, so he [Wigglesworth] simply acted on that Word by doing the same things with unquestioning faith and trust. He didn't analyze it, or intellectually dissect and decipher it. He had learned not to trust in what he knew or thought, but simply believe what God's Word said. In doing so, he saw thousands of miracles performed around the world through the use of anointed handkerchiefs. Paul wrote to the Corinthians that he feared that their minds might – 'be corrupted from the simplicity that is in Christ' (2 Corinthians 11:3). The point made by this verse is so important! Simply believe. It is surely a warning for us today, for it is so easy to complicate matters in our present society and lose that simplicity of faith.

> With reference to this point, *we note with interest that many more major miracles occur in the Global South, where the people have hardly been educated, than in the Western world.*

> Several different theories have been put forth about why this is. I believe one of the major reasons

is that the people in these nations simply believe and are healed, *while we, in our educated, over-intellectual, over-analytical Western world, all too often rationalize away faith for the miraculous.*

Jesus said, 'I thank You, Father, Lord of heaven and earth, because You have hidden these things from the wise and prudent, and have revealed them to babes' (Matthew 11:25). So many things are hidden from us through our supposed 'wisdom and prudence'. We must get back to simplicity.[132]

Too Great an Emphasis on Prayer?

Yes, you read the heading correctly! How could there be too great an emphasis on prayer? Particularly if we have previously identified prayer ministry as a legitimate means to the recovery of health? The point is this: *when we are praying, we are not doing.* Our Christian life must consist of prayer and activity. The author's observation is that God generally does not do for us that which we can do for ourselves. God did not supernaturally rescue Noah from a global deluge but, rather, gave him a hundred years of prior warning so that he could build an ark. When Jesus performed an outstanding miracle in raising Lazarus from the dead, He knew that the man's friends and family were perfectly capable of removing the redundant grave clothes, so there was no need to do so supernaturally (see John 11:44). An illustration worth considering is from the Exodus account:

---

132. Madden, pp.78-80.

As Pharaoh approached, the Israelites looked up, and there were the Egyptians, marching after them. They were terrified and cried out to the LORD. They said to Moses, 'Was it because there were no graves in Egypt that you brought us to the desert to die? What have you done to us by bringing us out of Egypt? Didn't we say to you in Egypt, "Leave us alone; let us serve the Egyptians"? It would have been better for us to serve the Egyptians than to die in the desert!' *Moses answered the people, 'Do not be afraid. Stand firm and you will see the deliverance the LORD will bring you today.* The Egyptians you see today you will never see again. *The LORD will fight for you; you need only to be still.'* Then the LORD said to Moses, *'Why are you crying out to me? Tell the Israelites to move on.* Raise your staff and stretch out your hand over the sea to divide the water so that the Israelites can go through the sea on dry ground. (Exodus 14:10-16, emphasis added)

Moses was crying out to God in prayer and telling the people to stand still and watch Him provide the miraculous means that would defeat the Egyptians. In fact, Moses had the miraculous means to deliver the people in his hand. Through his staff, the staff that had already been used to miraculous effect in the court of Pharaoh, leading up to this final exodus, and *God expected him to use it*. If we, as I believe is the case, have been given a 'staff' in the form of the spiritual gift of healing, why would we then need to cry out to God to do something for which we already have the means and the mandate[133] to accomplish? We would never pray, 'Lord, preach Your word to the people in my town,' because, as His followers, we have been commissioned to preach His word! And, in general,[134] He does not preach to individuals. Could it not be that His response many times when we pray for the sick may well be, 'Why are you crying out to me? Speak into the situation' (see Matthew 8:13), 'Lay your hands on the sick and they will recover' (see Mark 16:15-18). God ignores pragmatism and prescribes ways for things to be done. He had promised to Moses in the wilderness that He would dwell with the people of Israel through the Tabernacle, inside of which was the Ark of the Covenant, the symbol of His glory and presence. When David was crowned king of all Israel and subsequently set up his kingdom in Jerusalem, it was right for him to seek the presence of God and build a Tabernacle. It was right for him to place the Ark of the Covenant in that Tabernacle. It was not appropriate, however, to transport that Ark on a cattle-drawn wagon, however pragmatic that approach may have seemed. There was a prescribed mode of transportation, by poles on the shoulders of the priests. David did not follow the prescribed mode and there were negative, fatal consequences. As the cattle stumbled, Uzzah reached out and steadied the Ark. As a result, Uzzah was struck down dead as the instructions of Moses warned,[135] even though his intentions were honourable.[136] We must be careful in

---

133. Mark 16:15-18: to lay our 'hands on the sick, and they shall recover'.
134. 'Thousands of Muslims See Jesus in Dreams and Visions', Effective Faith, https://www.effectivefaith.co.uk/faith-media/testimonials/thousands-of-muslims-see-jesus-in-dreams-and-visions.html (accessed 3 September 2022). Possible exceptions in these last days. This site gives a selection of accounts and personal testimonies of Muslims who have come to faith in Jesus Christ as a result of Him appearing to them in a dream.
135. See Numbers 4:15.
136. See 2 Samuel 6:6-7.

the healing ministry that we use the means prescribed by God through the ministry of Jesus of Nazareth and His corresponding commissioning. *This thought does not deny that there are special cases where intercession is required on behalf of a sick person.* Jesus Himself warned that there is a type of spirit that causes illness and that does not come out except through prayer and fasting,[137] and as previously discussed, the healing ritual described in James 5 relies upon the faith of the elders and the prayers that are a consequence of that faith.

Lack of Personal Responsibility

In the same way that God will not intervene where the onus is on us to use our own initiative, equipping and anointing, He will generally not intervene to heal someone who has the ability to heal themselves through a change of lifestyle, such as eating a healthier diet, taking more exercise or quitting a harmful habit. One pastor tells of the lady in the healing line of his church asking for prayer for God to heal her of diabetes. Just before he began to pray, the Lord gave him an impression of the lady eating ice cream. He challenged her and asked her if she would be willing to give up the ice cream that she ate every night, to secure her healing? The lady admitted that her doctor had said much the same. The lady committed to give up ice cream and succeeded, and soon the diabetes was under control.

Similarly, we would not expect a smoker to be healed of bronchial disorders while he or she continued to use tobacco. However, often the release or deliverance from

---

137.   Matthew 17:19-21.

a bondage or addiction is a healing in itself, which in turn leads to an individual taking better care of their health, or indeed to a miraculous healing. A couple with whom the author is acquainted ran a bed-and-breakfast house in Bedfordshire, England. The man had smoked cigarettes for forty years prior to his conversion to Christianity, at which point he was convicted that he should quit. He had developed emphysema, which is a lung disease characterised by shortness of breath due to destruction and dilatation of the alveoli. His years of smoking had not helped this condition. He had joined a little Methodist church that practised a healing ministry. When he was ministered to, he was completely healed of his condition. Would God have healed him so miraculously had he still continued in the habit that had caused his disease?

Many pastors and church leaders are suffering stress-related ailments and are not being healed because they are not managing their lives in such a way as to reduce their stress. One obvious way is to observe a Sabbath rest. Sundays can be busy, but the way we are created calls out for us to rest one day in seven. When we ignore this biblical principle, we not only risk damaging our health but also hinder God's healing.

Geographical Impact

While the level of success experienced in the Christian healing ministry, particularly in the UK and in the Western world[138] in general, may not be comparable to the healing ministry of the New Testament, there are reports from

---

138. This may be an illusion since we can more easily check out what is local and what we know best.

other areas of the world claiming much greater levels of success.[139] The following illustrations provide anecdotal evidence of how geographical location appears to have a bearing on levels of success.

Reinhard Bonnke was a Pentecostal healing evangelist who latterly, with Daniel Kolenda, his successor, had ministered chiefly in the African continent. A large part of their time was spent ministering with Christ for all Nations (CfaN) in outdoor crusades.

Each month, the CfaN newsletter describes successes in terms of numbers of people who have come to personal faith in each crusade, but also regularly reports the healings of individuals from blindness, tumours and arthritic conditions. On several occasions, it has relayed how individuals have been raised from the dead.

In one of his yearly reviews, Bonnke wrote:

> This past year, we were awed by the unprecedented results of our campaigns in Gboko, Port Moresby, Uromi, Ogoja and Abuja: the salvations of hundreds of thousands, miracles of healings, deliverance and restoration.[140]

Yet when Bonnke came to Belfast's Odyssey (now the SSE) Arena several years ago, the number of people testifying to healing was very small. Additionally, the ailments from which they were healed appeared to the onlooker to be superficial. By contrast, there were many seriously ill people in attendance, some of whom were personal acquaintances

---

139. Wagner records how, at one of Carlos Annacondia's crusades in Argentina, a person with dwarfism is reported to have gained more than fifteen inches in height!
140. *IMPACT* 2001, a publication of evangelist Reinhard Bonnke (CfaN).

of the author. They sought healing, displayed exemplary faith and were disappointed. It is also true that not many people came to personal faith, despite powerful and 'evangelically sound'[141] preaching on the part of the evangelist.[142]

During the latter half of 2016, Reinhard Bonnke suffered severely following a cancer diagnosis and underwent the necessary treatment. He continued to minister online while Daniel Kolenda, his successor at CfaN, continued to preach to millions in Africa. Bonnke felt God directing him back to Africa for one last great opportunity. After a period of renewed health and strength, Bonnke returned for a final crusade.

Shortly afterwards, Bonnke passed away.

Until his retirement some years ago, Paul Reid was senior pastor of Christian Fellowship Church, Belfast's largest neo-Pentecostal denomination and one with which the name of the Christian worship leader and songwriter Robin Mark is associated. With his permission, I include how he recalled,[143] immediately before leaving India on one occasion, he and a colleague had had a short amount of time to pray with a chronically sick local man. He was

---

141. By strict Northern Ireland standards!
142. It is not presently known by the author how successful Bonnke's healing ministry was in his native Germany; however, by way of encouragement to the reader and as the exception to the rule being emphasised in this section, Bill Johnson (Bethel Church, Redding, California) records how he saw a miraculous healing while ministering in Germany. As he prayed before the meeting, he had an impression in his mind of a woman, with an arthritic spine, to his right as he preached and him declaring the Lord's healing over her. He writes: 'When it came time for the meeting, I asked was there anyone there with arthritis of the spine. A woman to my right waved her hand. I had her stand up and declared over her *"The Lord Jesus heals you!"* I then asked her where was her pain? She wept saying: "It is impossible, but it is gone!"' (Johnson, pp.140-141).
143. This is a précis of a portion of a sermon preached by Pastor Paul Reid in St Anne's Cathedral, Belfast, in 2005.

a Hindu man who had seen their previous meetings advertised and, consequently, he was requesting prayer for the healing of throat cancer. It was four months before Pastor Reid received a letter from India confirming that the man with whom he and his colleague had prayed had been completely healed, and had since become a Christian! Excited by this news Paul made an appeal at the forthcoming Sunday service at his church in Belfast for the sick to come forward for healing as he and this same colleague ministered to them. To the great disappointment of the two men, no one was instantaneously healed. Paul used this experience on the occasion mentioned to illustrate the fact that Christians have the responsibility to minister to the sick, but it is God who heals, as and when He chooses. This incident, however, further illustrates how geography may have affected the success of the healing.

Eddie Dorrans was a Presbyterian minister in County Antrim, Northern Ireland, and is now enjoying retirement. While visiting South Korea, he was compelled to pray for a sick baby in the congregation. Immediately he laid his hands on the child, it ceased crying. It was later confirmed that the child had been healed instantaneously. Back home in Ballycastle, however, despite valiant efforts, Eddie struggled to see the fruits of a healing ministry during his time there, a ministry that he attempted to extend beyond his own congregation to the other churches of the town.

Bill Prankard is a Pentecostal pastor from Ottawa, Canada. He ministers regularly in healing in North America. He personally cites the Toronto Airport Christian Fellowship Church as a location where he has been instrumental in the healing of many individuals over a sustained period of time. The author has heard him preaching there. This is Bill's account of the healing, in Toronto, of a man from Bangor, County Down, the town of the author's home church:

> George McMurtry was a believer from Northern Ireland. He'd had 5 strokes. His left leg was withered to half its size, and his left arm was withered and curved up and of no use to him. He could only walk by using canes to drag himself along very painfully . . . George never accepted that his condition was permanent. He always said, 'I believe that God is going to heal me.'

> I was at Toronto Airport Assembly ministering along with others at a conference on healing. George had persuaded some people from his church to bring him all the way from Ireland to the conference . . .

> I gave a message, and at the end of the message, I said, 'God is healing people, and anyone who needs healing should stand.' George stood up along with many others. I said, 'Put your hand wherever you need healing.' George heard me say, 'Take your left hand and put it on your head.' . . . Then, I said, 'Someone's hand is being healed.' At that moment, George's withered left hand suddenly fell away and his arm straightened out of its curved, half-moon position and began to move freely. His fingers and hands were moving for the first time in 5 years!

> George's friends told him to go up to the platform and show everyone what God had done for him.

He was halfway down the aisle when his friends called after him, 'George you forgot your cane!' Previously, he could not have walked 5 steps without his cane, but George kept going because he didn't need his cane. As he walked, his leg braces, which were held on by Velcro, fell open and came off. By the time he got to the front, his withered, paralyzed leg was totally healed, and George was completely restored . . .

When George returned home to Ireland, his doctor checked him, and said, 'This is a miracle. There is no other explanation.' The local paper wrote it up and put it on the front page. Even better, George started his own ministry and today he is vigorous and active in the Lord's service. Even though I have seen thousands of miracles by now, each time it is as awesome and wonderful as the first.[144]

Now George himself takes up the story:

Returning home, I'll never forget the look on [my wife] Betty's face. She had been wary when I had rung to tell her what happened but she couldn't deny the change when she saw me in person. Since then I haven't looked back. My medication was stopped, the hospital tests came back clear and I've been well ever since, but it was a long and a difficult journey. There were times when I thought I couldn't keep going, couldn't face another day. I had questioned God, cried to Him, and been angry with Him. Yet there was always a quiet voice inside telling me to keep going, and keep going, and keep going. In the end, despite the tears and the setbacks, the dark days and long nights, God kept His promise. I have been healed.

Yet the year after George's undeniable miraculous healing, Bill was invited to George's own church, Bangor Elim Pentecostal Church, to minister. Bill laid hands on some seriously ill people known personally to the author and pronounced their healing. Some continue to have their illnesses and several have since died as a result of their ailments.

The author can testify personally to this geographical healing enigma, as recorded in his journal:

On my most recent trip to Cali, Colombia, our team was conducting meetings with a healing emphasis in two locations at opposite sides of the city. As my colleague and myself arrived at our venue we could see evidence of need, as our first sight of the inside of the church was a lady in a wheelchair. We engaged in typically energetic (and loud) Colombian praise and worship and we both spoke a word from the scriptures. We each had an interpreter and as we ministered to separate lines of individuals, I saw that the lady in the wheelchair was in my line. However, I heard some commotion in the other line and realised that my colleague was witnessing something out of the ordinary. Later on, at the end of the meeting the pastor of the church shared with several of us that as my colleague had prayed with a baby with a physical disability, the child's leg had visibly grown out by as much as two inches! Whilst the parents were overjoyed at what certainly appeared to be a miracle, my colleague had missed the moment. He had been praying with his eyes closed (as many of us have been taught to do despite there being no scriptural basis – it is recommended by many who teach prayer ministry, that those who are praying with individuals should of necessity have their eyes open, paying careful attention to the body movements and facial expressions of the individual being ministered to, as the ministry takes place). Anyway, as we rejoiced after the service had been formally closed, I noticed across the room that the lady in the wheelchair with whom I had prayed was sobbing. I asked my interpreter to come with me to affirm that healing is not always instantaneous. Her reply surprised me as it was relayed to me. I had not properly understood her condition during the ministry time. She had been suffering from cancer and her treatment had left her weakened and needing the help of a wheelchair. She had come to the meeting knowing she had a malignant tumour in one of her breasts. She had felt a burning sensation during the ministry time and upon checking, she reported that the lump had now gone! She was weeping with joy! Two outstanding interventions of healing had taken place, perhaps more, that we never got to hear about. Despite the expectation, neither of us had seen that consistency at home. Why should this be the case?

As we probe further into the impact of geography on the success of our healing ministries, it is fair to observe that in our post-modern Western world many contemporary Christians are at the limit of their belief in the supernatural when they accept the possibility of God healing them spiritually through the finished work of Jesus Christ. Where physical healing is concerned, it is a 'bridge too far' because many can't get beyond the designation of Jesus as the Saviour. This may be considered similar to the phenomenon previously referred to – that Jesus Himself experienced in His home town of Nazareth. He could do no mighty miracle in that place because the people there could not get beyond the fact that He was the carpenter, the son of Joseph. Mark 8:22-26 records an incident where Jesus took a blind man out of the town of Bethsaida before He healed him. Does this not seem unusual? This appeared to be a particularly challenging healing that happened in stages rather than in the more common instantaneous fashion. A clue to the incident may be found in Luke 10:13, which indicates that although Jesus evidently had performed miraculous works there during the course of His public ministry, Bethsaida was akin to Nazareth in its deliberate unbelief.[145] Jesus proclaimed:

> Woe to you, Chorazin! Woe to you, Bethsaida! For if the miracles that were performed in you had been performed in Tyre and Sidon, they would have repented long ago, sitting in sackcloth and ashes.

145. Warrington states that lack of faith does not restrict Jesus, but rather Jesus chooses not to heal because of an absence of faith. He goes on to say that the identity of unbelief is rejection, not doubt.

This train of thought leads us to the subject of territorial spirits, i.e. spirits that have acquired a certain legal jurisdiction over specific geographical areas. In the Early Church era, Origen[146] conceded that there were places where demons exercised considerable spiritual power especially in so-called 'holy places', where curious spells had been administered. He saw the possibility of specific demons controlling entire geographical areas to rule 'those who have subjected themselves to evil'.[147] Woolmer suggests that although the New Testament does not specifically teach that Satan's organised structure of principalities and powers have territorial authority, there are several incidents in the gospels that support such a theology. In addition to the examples of Nazareth and Bethsaida cited above, he notes that the spirits occupying the Gadarene demoniac begged Jesus not to send them out of the region. This area, known as the Decapolis, may have been in particular spiritual bondage. Surprisingly, unlike other individuals who came to faith in Him, Jesus did not call the man formerly known as Legion to follow Him. Rather He instructed him to remain in the locality, testifying to Jesus' power over the demonic, thereby shedding light, and weakening the spiritual strongholds over the region. By way of contrast, the formerly blind man of Bethsaida was told not to return to the village. The possibility of the existence of territorial spirits certainly helps to explain not only why healing appears to take place in greater proportion and with greater intensity in some places as opposed to others, even when the same people are ministering, but also why some places are more open to respond to evangelistic effort than others.

---

146. Origen of Alexandria (c. AD 184–c.253), also known as Origen Adamantius.
147. Woolmer, p.164, citing Henry Chadwick.

Acceptance of this notion of territorial spirits is not to detract from the sovereignty or omnipotence of God, but rather to emphasise the fact that where individuals and races have deliberately subjected themselves to evil, God gives them over to their evil ways.[148] And so they, and potentially their geographical surroundings, offspring, buildings, etc., fall under Satan's jurisdiction, although not to such an extent as to be unredeemable. The inability of Christians to acknowledge, recognise and overcome these 'principalities' and 'powers',[149] together with the 'spiritual forces of wickedness in the heavenly places',[150] may contribute substantially to instances of non-healing in particular communities despite the sincere individual faith of those attempting to minister healing.

The author has previously mentioned Paul Bennison and has also included one of his sermon outlines by way of reference. Despite being a relatively unknown English itinerant minister, Paul has shared church platforms with others who have had well-known international healing ministries. In his travels (to more than a hundred countries), he has testified to having seen miracles in Eastern Europe, India, China and Latin America, including instances of cancers disappearing and limbs growing from stumps. Paul is a good reference point when considering the geographical impact on healing 'success' because he is both global, on account of his travels, and local, because up until recently he lived literally just down the road from the author. Paul confirms that the miraculous is prevalent in China, India and South America, and cites both the faith of church

---

148. See Romans 1:24-32 for a similar concept.
149. Ephesians 6:12(a) KJV.
150. Ephesians 6:12(b) NASB.

leaders and the faith of the individuals needing healing to be significant factors in the success of a healing ministry. Paul recalls a visit to China, when the pastor was very keen to introduce him to two particular Chinese ladies. When Paul enquired as to who they were, he was furnished with an account of how, on separate occasions, they had both died and been raised to life. On one visit to West Church, prior to moving to Bangor, Paul opened the meeting up for healing ministry. One significant reported success was the immediate marked improvement in a young child suffering from severe autism, with the prognosis that he would never be able to communicate properly. There was not, however, a complete healing that evening and therefore, according to those who oppose the continuance of the healing gifts, this did not represent a successful New Testament miraculous healing. Nevertheless, this incident proved to be the start of a journey that would lead this child to develop and learn how to communicate, win a place at the local grammar school and university, and to ponder theology! In a church interview with the young man's mother, the author recalled how, on one occasion, as a young boy some way into his journey to wholeness, he had considered which was the saddest event in human history: the fall of man or the crucifixion of Christ! Profound for a child who, according to experts, would never have the capacity to communicate!

Paul tells how, in a cathedral in Scandinavia, God was moving powerfully as he went around ministering to the sick. There were three wheelchair-bound individuals sitting together, and as two of them got up and walked, Paul said (through his interpreter) to the third who had witnessed the previous two healings: 'Your faith must be strong for healing now also?' The man replied: 'What will happen to my benefits?' Paul answered very frankly: 'You won't need them, sir; you will be able to work.' Sadly, the man refused any healing intervention! This account leads us into our next section.

Healing Hindered By Wrong Attitudes

There are attitudes on the part of individuals who are ill that may hinder their healing. An obvious one is lack of personal faith, although it is clear from earlier arguments that the necessity of faith often lies with the person or persons administering the healing. In the event where healing is not instantaneous and complete, those opposed to the Pentecostal theology of Christian healing claim this as proof that the New Testament spiritual gift of healing has been withdrawn and thus is not in operation. Those involved in ministering the gift of healing, however, emphasise the need to receive the healing on the basis of personal faith, even if the onset of healing is not immediately obvious. This is the test of faith, for 'without faith it is impossible to please God' (Hebrews 11:6), and more relevant with regard to healing:

> But when you ask [God for anything that is lacking, e.g. healing], you must believe and not doubt, because the one who doubts is like a wave of the sea, blown and tossed about by the wind. That person should not expect to receive anything from the Lord. (James 1:6-7)

James' epistle emphasises the practical outworkings of faith as being proof that real inner faith actually exists. Many see this practical emphasis as the element that is essential before Christian healing can take place. It is also a feature of 'holding on to one's healing'. Critics of healing campaigns often accuse organisers of emotionally charging the atmosphere to create a sense of well-being akin to the 'improvement' experienced by many while in the doctor's or dentist's waiting room. Often individuals testify to their 'healing' only to find that when the emotional atmosphere dies down, or when they return to a mundane environment, the ailment returns. Whereas others see this as the devil testing the individual, a situation where continued health requires a positive attitude of faith despite the apparent return of the illness. Many healing campaigns may appear to have been unsuccessful, therefore, because individuals are lacking in the continuing faith required to sustain their healing.

A similar problem can occur where too much dependence is placed upon the medical practitioners and their diagnoses. This amounts to what in essence is a wrong object of faith – a form of idolatry. This problem can range from accepting an inadvertent 'curse' through believing statements[151] such as 'You will never walk again'; 'You will never be any better than this'; 'You have six months to live'; etc., through to over-dependency on medicines or the regime of continued nursing care.[152] There is, nevertheless, some support for using medicines in Scripture. Hezekiah, although his healing had been confirmed by the prophet Isaiah, was still required to use medication in the form of a poultice before that healing became effective; Timothy was encouraged to use a little wine for medicinal purposes; Jesus himself refers to the use of the standard medical remedy of oil and wine in the parable of the good Samaritan, and He said: 'It

---

151. Particularly where these statements involve authority figures.
152. See also footnote #102 by way of contrast.

is not the healthy who need a doctor, but those who are ill' (Luke 5:31).

> Beware of those who say turning to medicine and medics is a contradiction to faith and prayer. Did not the Good Samaritan care for the one lying ill on the side of the road? Didn't Paul exhort Timothy to take wine for the sake of his stomach? Are we not to use the natural means that God has given to us which help our bodies' restoration to health? Of course we are – we are not to neglect the temple of the Holy Spirit! It seems at times that we treat our bodies as enemies rather than temples, with our unhealthy living.[153]

Bethel Church in Redding, California, claims a significant geographical success in ministering miraculous healing. Nevertheless, Kris Vallotton (co-founder of Bethel School of Supernatural Ministry) states in the context of his friend, co-worker and founder of the Bethel Healing Rooms, Paul Manwaring, not being healed supernaturally 'the miracle never came'[154] but, rather, he was healed through medical means.

> Paul's recovery opened a door of revelation to us. We began to understand that miracles happen in different ways. Although God often heals people through prayer, there are other times the Great Physician chooses to co-labor with His medical interns to see wholeness restored to the life of His people.[155]

---

153. McKelvey, extracted from a Master of Theology essay, answering the question: 'Outline (with your reasons) a pastoral approach to someone who has not been healed despite the services of a healing ministry'.
154. Manwaring endorsements by Kris Vallotton.
155. Manwaring endorsements by Kris Valloton.

In support of formal medical treatments, much is made of Saint Paul's association with Luke, whom he refers to as the 'beloved physician' (Colossians 4:14 KJV) and who gave us the Gospel of Luke and the book of Acts. However, David Foot makes the observation that when Luke was present during a particular emergency, he did not minister practical assistance himself. The event is recorded in Acts 20:7-12 and involves the fall of Eutychus to his death and mentioned in a previous section (see pages 71-72). It is delivered to us by Luke in the first person, yet it does not appear to involve him; neither do the events occurring on Malta with Publius' father-in-law, the bite by the poisonous snake and the mass healing of the islanders (Acts 28:1-10). Foot goes on to say how, in 2 Chronicles 16, it is recorded that King Asa suffered a disease in his last years and died because he was unwilling to seek God for healing but turned rather to the physicians (see v.12). He goes on to cite Job 13:4, which says, 'Ye are forgers of lies, ye are all physicians of no value' (KJV). He concludes: 'There is no commendation of the professional healers in the Old Testament',[156] and on the basis of the account of the haemorrhaging woman who had suffered many things of physicians and, rather, had grown worse, he states 'The New Testament is similar'.[157]

By way of contrast, Manwaring states, with profound impact from his personal experience, that 'surgery is not a second-class healing'.[158] He further states:

---

156. Foot, David R.P., *Divine Healing in the Scriptures* (Worthing: Henry E. Walter, 1969), p.47.
157. Foot, p. 47.s
158. Manwaring, p.32.

> Those [cancer] treatments are often heavenly revelations given to men and women to help destroy this disease, both medically and surgically, in the absence of a divine miracle.[159]

Another seemingly obvious condition hindering healing is the lack of a desire to be healed. The man at the Pool of Bethesda had an infirmity for thirty-eight years. Jesus was passing that way and, seeing him, asked, 'Do you want to get well?' (John 5:6). It is surprising how many sick people depend on their condition to seek attention and achieve significance; who thrive on self-pity or are reluctant to accept the responsibilities of good health, including working and the surrender of income benefits, like the man encountered by Paul Bennison in Scandinavia, as previously cited on page 137. His benefit payments were more important to him than his mobility. Indeed, many in today's society consider themselves to be fortunate when they receive an incapacitation if it means the possibility of a successful industrial or insurance claim. The devil, as the master of deception, has manipulated the human psyche to the point of orchestrating such conditions as:

- Munchausen's syndrome, where individuals pretend to exhibit symptoms of serious diseases to gain sympathy and attention;
- Hypochondria, where serious disease is feared and suspected although rarely is present;
- Psychosomatic ailments, which have all the real symptoms but with no underlying disease present.

---

159. Manwaring, p.119.

Lack of Prayer

Having challenged the reader to engage in activity rather than simply to pray, we must also examine what part prayer plays in healing when it is appropriate. When praying about any set of circumstances, we are encouraged to 'pray in the Spirit on all occasions with all kinds of prayers and requests' (Ephesians 6:18). Also, 'We do not know what we ought to pray for, but the Spirit himself intercedes for us through wordless groans' (Romans 8:26-27). The majority of Charismatics and Pentecostals believe that both of these passages refer in some measure to the use of the spiritual gift of tongues. The practice of praying in tongues is therefore often considered an important feature when praying for the sick, both with and without an interpretation, depending on the setting. The most important factor in praying for the sick, however (as with praying for anything), is persistence; the need to 'Pray without ceasing' (1 Thessalonians 5:17 KJV). Jesus' parable of the widow seeking justice and the neighbour asking for loaves at midnight makes this fact abundantly clear (Luke 11:5-8), as does Jesus' exhortations for us to 'ask, seek and knock', which are written in the present continuous tense: 'Go on asking, go on seeking, go on knocking . . .' (see Matthew 7:7). Lack of persistence and even lack of application in prayer may be a major cause of failure in the healing ministry. It is noteworthy in the life of Christ that He often rose before the working day began and spent time in prayer, thus when the occasion for healing arose, He was already intimately aware of the situation through His communion with the Father. Each healing He performed was well immersed in prayer prior to His touch or spoken word of rebuke to the ailment. When a local church or a community is bereft of a meaningful prayer life, then the entire scope of its ministry suffers. In the same way as it is unlikely to see many converts to Christianity, it is unlikely to have major successes in terms of Christian healing.

Let there be a word of warning here. There are healing declarations that the author does not like to hear, although they are used regularly by those involved in the ministry of Christian healing:

> 'I command pain to go in Jesus' name ...'
>
> 'Pain, I bind you and command you to leave ...'
>
> 'I curse pain ...' etc., etc.

Pain is a gift from God; it shows us there is something physically wrong. Pain may be causing distress but it is not the enemy. What if we touched something hot enough to harm our human tissue but did not feel the pain to produce the reaction to quickly remove the body part from the proximity of the hot item? Congenital insensitivity to pain with anhidrosis (CIPA), also known as hereditary sensory and autonomic neuropathy type IV, is a hereditary disease which renders the sufferer unable to feel pain and heat. It is therefore possible for the sufferer to sustain significant injuries without knowing. What if our misguided prayers were potentially inflicting a sort of spiritual CIPA on the already ill person being ministered to? What if the pain were to leave but the underlying cause had not been dealt with? The person who had been ministered to would continue to believe that he or she had been healed, without having any indicator that the condition could be in fact worsening. Why, you say, would God take away the pain in answer to prayer and leave the lingering ailment? Answer: *He would not!* If our foremost premise in this section is correct, however, we are confronting a spiritual enemy. When we pray or declare something that is against the express will of God (and I believe these kinds of statement are), it is possible that the devil can have legal rights over the statement. God will not answer a prayer that is against His will, but the devil might!

When It Is God's Will Not to Heal

Joni Eareckson-Tada has been a quadriplegic since she experienced an injury during a diving accident while in her teens. Despite seeking healing from all legitimate sources, she has never been healed. She has nevertheless helped countless long-term sufferers through the inspiration given in her numerous books and personal letters to those having suffered similar injuries.[160] Is it God's will for her not to be healed because of the empathetic ministry she now has? Are there specific ailments that God just does not choose to heal? Despite his experience in numerous successful healing ventures within the Anglican Church, Woolmer states:

> I would add that there is very little evidence of those being born with severe mental illness ever being healed . . . if this is correct, then it poses sharp questions for the sort of theology . . . which encourages us to claim healing as a theological right.[161]

160. Masters, p.225.
161. Woolmer, p.244.

If, however, Woolmer is correct in his assessment, then the New Testament spiritual gift of healing is similarly in question on the basis that Jesus and the apostles appeared to encounter mental conditions of this kind regularly and heal them with a word or a touch.

While we reserve our judgement on whether Paul's thorn was an illness, based on the earlier arguments in this work, many use his situation of enjoying sufficiency of grace as an example to those who are suffering chronic or terminal illness. As Dickinson puts it:

> Not only was [Paul's] healing refused but it was clearly established by God that the 'thorn', while being a 'messenger of Satan', was specifically intended and used to provide spiritual benefit and blessing through the discipline it imposed and the grace it evoked.[162]

So, in Paul's case, to pray for the sick (as he himself had done on three occasions) clearly was to oppose God's will, at least for Paul. Lawrence, however, in support of the prayer 'Thy will be done' being prayed during healing prayer, believes that this phrase is not 'a sigh of resignation. It is more like a battle-cry'. He believes God's will is for wholeness, that a call for His will to be done invokes His power to rebuke 'all that is alien to the perfection of His creative purpose – cleaning, purging, recreating, making whole!'[163]

---

162. Dickinson, p.108.
163. Lawrence, pp.68-69.

Summary

In a sense, it is easy to offer an excuse for every case of non-healing, one that is both plausible and biblical. This work, however, has pleaded with the author for it to be *more than a catalogue of qualified failure on behalf of the Church*. We are living in an increasingly secular and unbelieving society. At every opportunity, it criticises the Church on account of its relevancy, its intolerances, its dogmatism, its alleged hypocrisy, and on account of the cross and the very Person of Christ. Truly, the world can be charged with 'Christophobia'! The Church of the 1st century may have been persecuted and hated on account of the person of Christ, but it was nevertheless relevant; it ministered in signs and wonders. Those in government took note of the apostles that they had been with Christ; that they emulated Christ. They were Christians — Christ-ones. They exuded Christ. Is there a Church-wide answer to the question of non-healing outside of those hindrances believed to be genuine by the author and cited above?

Conclusion

⚬———⟨o⟩———⚬

Notwithstanding the previous summary paragraph, it is difficult to reach a definitive conclusion on the successes and failures of Christian healing based on Scripture, conviction and experience. It would also be vain on the part of the author to contemplate that the superficial study that this work represents should reveal the solution to what may amount to be an 1,800-year-old problem. It is important to recognise that there is much study still to be done, and that the foregoing examination is restricted by the nature and present purpose of this work. In support of the need for further study, we may quote Elwell:

> The kind of ailments that were healed in the New Testament period, the nature and place of faith, the significance of suffering in God's economy, the importance of the subconscious and its influence on the body, the relations between gifts of healing and medical science . . . these have not received the attention they require today.[164]

We must, nevertheless, admit that it is difficult to apply a consistent exegesis of the New Testament and reach the conclusion that the gift of healing was withdrawn long ago because it somehow became superfluous early in the

---

164. Elwell, p.1043.

Church era. Doing so not only weakens our commission as members and ministers of the Church to preach the gospel, but it also makes sections of the New Testament redundant to contemporary Christianity, and calls for a theology of 'micro-dispensationalism'. We have built a theology of healing that matches our experience of healing, rather than exercising faith and expecting the miraculous. There is some value in Warrington's assessment of Jesus' ministry as being evidently unique; however, when Jesus of Nazareth embarked on His public ministry, He did not spend a lot of time addressing what we still consider to be the great evils in the world. He didn't for instance wage war against poverty – and there was plenty of it in 1st-century Israel ('The poor you will always have', Matthew 26:11) – He didn't, notably, address societal injustice, global hunger and the like. The Kingdom that He proclaimed would deal with these issues, as we understand from Scripture, and the Church that He birthed through the Holy Spirit, at the first Feast of Pentecost after His ascension, has gone on to make advances against all of these global issues. And, in a sense, these issues did not need supernatural intervention. They are all problems for which society has been responsible and which society can fix, given sufficient effort and correct motivation. Jesus therefore chose not to make these issues part of His earthly ministry, but not so with sickness.

Our Obligation to Heal

John 9:5 records that Jesus stated: 'While I am in the world, I am the light of the world.' This means that Matthew 5:14, 'You [disciples] are the light of the world', should be understood as being a continuum of Christ's ministry. And while Jesus said we would do greater things than He did, no doubt through His ministry of intercession with the Father, He did not specifically call us to calm storms, walk on water,[165] multiply food, turn water into wine,[166] and similar miracles,[167] but He *did* call us to heal the sick, and we must acknowledge that in the main we have failed.

Many scholars and writers have their individual theories with regard to the lack of success and we have looked at some of these in the section above. It is perhaps not surprising that outstanding miracles are lacking where unbelief is fostered among Church leaders. As Wimber says, 'If we believe in a theology that does not include the possibility of contemporary Christians doing the work of Jesus . . . we will not have a practice of signs and wonders.'[168] According to Woolmer, in the account of the epileptic boy, Jesus gave three reasons for the initial lack of success: lack of prayer (and fasting), lack of faith, and the prevailing spiritual climate,[169] whereas Wimber attributes lack of healing to insufficient faith, concealed sin, disunity in the Church, faulty diagnosis, or a lack of persistence in prayer.[170] Such understandings give little comfort to a sincere Christian who has persistently sought healing with supposed faith. There is, nevertheless, a strong suggestion from the New Testament accounts and from contemporary reports of miraculous healings in other parts of the world, that if we can get the conditions for

---

165. Although it is a worthwhile exercise for the reader to research miracles recorded by Mel Tari during the Indonesian revival in the 1960s.
166. Again, see the work of Mel Tari.
167. Paul nevertheless lists those who are 'workers of miracles' as having an office within the local church.
168. Wimber, *Power Evangelism*, p.95.
169. Woolmer, p.242.
170. Wimber, John, *Power Healing* (London: Hodder & Stoughton, 1986), p.164.

revival right, then we will also have the right conditions for a successful healing ministry. These conditions would appear to be an atmosphere of prayer, a spirit of Christian unity and a community of faith. And while there is evidence of the power of the gift of healing being stronger in various geographical locations, there is not strong scriptural proof of a theology of territorial spirits. Rather, community faith is weakened through an inaccurate community world-view.

Pastoral Issues

There is a need to carefully pastor those who have had the expectation for healing and have not been healed, and also those who have been bereaved despite their loved ones having availed of a healing ministry. For the first of these groups, it must be borne in mind that while the sick person is still alive, a future opportunity for healing can almost always exist. Right until the end. And beyond? We have already made reference not only to the raising from the dead of individuals by the Old Testament prophets, by Jesus and by the apostles but also in our lifetime. For our encouragement to believe in the miraculous, it is worth including another testimony from the ministry of Smith Wigglesworth:

> She lay motionless on the bed. The very scent of death seemed to fill the room. For many months, the tumour had sapped away both her life and her will. Once, all she had wanted was to live for her children, but the pain had become unbearable. Now it seemed that there was no hope.
>
> Awakened early by the excruciating throbbing that racked her entire body, she now lay praying

against her old familiar enemy. She had nothing else left. No longer did she have the strength to move or cry out even if she desired to. Even though she believed that she could be healed, she couldn't help thinking that this day would be her last. Life could have been wonderful, but life like this wasn't worth living. A loud knock at the door interrupted her thoughts.

Mr Fisher, an elder from her church, quietly announced, 'I've brought someone to see you. This is Mr Wigglesworth. He's going to pray for you.' Out of the corner of her eye, she caught a glimpse of him, an older man with a grey moustache and a twinkle in his eye. A definite air of authority was about him as he spoke. She sensed his love of Jesus. 'I know you are very weak, but if you wish to be healed and cannot lift your arm, or move at all, it might be possible that you can raise your finger.' Something about this man, the strange air of authority, even the tone of his voice, seemed to spark faith in her. 'Yes, yes, I do want to be healed! I must let him know,' tumbled through her mind. With every bit of strength she could muster, she concentrated on raising her index finger. As the men stared intently, they almost missed the slight shift.

Suddenly everything changed. The pain had vanished. She wasn't in her bedroom any more, but was surrounded by countless numbers of people and such glorious singing. And there was Jesus. Oh, how lovely He is, she thought. His face shone with a light that lit up everything. 'She's dead. She's dead.' Mr Fisher was panic stricken, his face contorted with fear. He had brought Wigglesworth, hoping that she might be healed, and now she had died. What would people think? He slumped in a chair with his face in his hands, moaning, 'Oh, what shall I do?' While Mr Fisher groaned, Wigglesworth tossed back the covers, reached into the bed, and pulled her out. Carrying her lifeless body across the room, he propped it up against the wall. There was no pulse, no breath. She was absolutely dead. He looked into her face, and sternly commanded, 'In the name of Jesus, I rebuke death.' Mr Fisher looked up in amazement. Was he absurd? What was he doing? Before he could say a word, her whole body began to tremble. 'In the name of Jesus, I command you to walk.' All she knew was that Jesus looked directly at her and pointed. Oh, what a beautiful time she'd been having, but as Jesus looked at her, she knew she had to go back for the children. Jesus faded from view as she suddenly heard, 'In the name of Jesus, in the name of Jesus, walk!' She awoke to find herself walking across her bedroom floor. She felt strong and alive! The pain was gone, the tumour had disappeared. Mr Fisher stood with his mouth wide open, just staring at her.

That night the astonished doctor sat in the congregation as she told her remarkable story. She would never forget her visit to heaven, nor the visit from the man with the twinkle in his eye and the faith in his words, Smith Wigglesworth.

And so, she was 'rescued'[171] from beyond the brink at precisely the right time, and there is certainly much scriptural evidence that God's timing is of paramount importance in His dealings with humankind. It is those individuals who wait upon the Lord who will renew their strength (Isaiah 40:31). The psalmist says, 'I waited patiently for the LORD' (Psalm 40:1). Patience[172] is one of the fruits of the Spirit listed by Paul the apostle, and faithfulness and persistence are essential Christian qualities highlighted by Jesus during His earthly ministry. Biblical patience is closely linked with hope; 'wait' is translated 'hope' in the NIV rendering of the previously cited Isaiah passage, and so replacing the disappointment in the individual with hope should always be a pastoral goal.

For the second group, in the case where a person has died (and has not been raised, nor is there that prospect), it would seem wise to counsel loved ones on the basis of the infinite well-being of the deceased, where no further illness, pain or suffering is present, 'For the old order of things has passed away' (Revelation 21:4). It should also be stressed that *an apparent lack of faith to be healed does not indicate a lack of faith for salvation.*

Many of the opponents of the present-day ministry of miraculous divine healing (a representative sample of whom

---

171. Rescued hardly seems the correct term for being removed from the immediate presence of Jesus!
172. The head-on collision of a gospel that promotes the spiritual fruit of patience with an age that expects instant gratification, from its coffee to its cash to its credit to its internet access, is unlikely to produce a plethora of instantaneous healing miracles.

has been quoted in this work) have emphasised the alleged devastating effects that failed healing attempts have had on individuals. Yet, even where healings of the calibre described in the gospels and Acts have not taken place, rather than the individuals being disappointed, it is only on rare occasions that the ministry of healing prayer does not help significantly. John Dundee, once Professor of Anaesthetics at Queen's University, Belfast, undertook a piece of research involving apparent miraculous healing claims made by thirty-two people who had attended the Centre for Christian Renewal in Rostrevor, Northern Ireland. While he, like many others previously cited, 'Failed to find undisputed evidence of miraculous healing', he comments:

> As a result of this survey I would commend rather than criticise the role of the church in healing the whole person . . . I *did* meet patients who were improved in mind and spirit.[173]

The theology of Christian healing also brings challenges to our own personal Christianity. If the ability to 'lay hands on the sick, and they shall recover' applies to all who believe in the apostles' message in all generations, then we, as Christians in whatever era of the Church age, have an obligation to participate. We must therefore prayerfully examine our lives and belief systems for such barriers and hindrances as those listed above, so that we may be a part of His Kingdom coming and His will being done on earth as it is in heaven.

---

173. Masters, pp.215-216, quotes Dundee. This is a decidedly positive statement to have been cited by such a protagonist in the opposition of contemporary healing movements.

Not the End

This is where the author may have concluded this work; however, it leaves the Christian believer, as many literary Christian works do, concluding that the writer has not presented enough evidence in his argument to represent proof for his assertion. In this case, that assertion would be that healing is available through the Church and that the supernatural gift of healing is still in operation, or that we do not and/or cannot know why there is such a lack of generally observed success in the Church's present healing ministry. And so the author is led to be more exhaustive in concluding this work.

Addendum

The Great Decommission

Decommissioning is a general term for a formal process to withdraw something from an active status.

> When a power company decides to close a nuclear power plant permanently, the facility must be decommissioned by safely removing it from service and reducing residual radioactivity to a level that permits release of the property and termination of the operating license. The Nuclear Regulatory Commission has strict rules governing nuclear power plant decommissioning, involving clean-up of radioactively contaminated plant systems and structures, and removal of the radioactive fuel. These requirements protect workers and the public during the entire decommissioning process and the public after the license is terminated.[174]

And in the author's own part of the world, it has generally related to the putting away of illegal weapons beyond use.

> 'The decommissioning of the arms of the IRA is now an accomplished fact,' said John

174 United States Nuclear Regulatory Commission, https://www.ourenergypolicy.org/wp-content/uploads/2015/11/decommissioning.pdf (Page 1)

de Chastelain, the retired Canadian general who had been responsible for overseeing the decommissioning process since 1997. 'This can be the end of the use of the gun in Irish politics,' he added. He presented a confidential report on his weapons inspections to the British and Irish governments following several months of decommissioning activity involving both sides of the Irish border concluding: 'The arms involved included the full range of ammunition, rifles, machine guns, mortars, handguns, explosives, explosive substances and other arms.'

For the first time, IRA members present at the decommissioning declared that all their weapons had been put beyond use and the then Irish Taoiseach Bertie Ahern said that the decommissioning was a 'landmark development'. 'Today is a momentous day for the people of this island,' he said. 'Many believed this day would never come. Many believe it should have happened a long time ago. But it has now come. We cannot forget our sad and tragic past, but we must now look forward . . . I call on everyone to now seize the opportunity that is opening in front of us to build a better Ireland.'[175]

The instruction of Jesus that we refer to as the Great Commission, and that we accept as the Church's mandate, follows, as recorded by the evangelists Matthew and Mark respectively:

---

175.   'IRA Arms Decommissioned', *The Guardian*, 26 September 2005.

Then the eleven disciples went to Galilee, to the mountain where Jesus had told them to go. When they saw him, they worshipped him; but some doubted. Then Jesus came to them and said, 'All authority in heaven and on earth has been given to me. Therefore go and make disciples of all nations, baptising them in the name of the Father and of the Son and of the Holy Spirit, and teaching them to obey everything I have commanded you. And surely I am with you always, to the very end of the age.' (Matthew 28:16-20)

Later Jesus appeared to the Eleven as they were eating; he rebuked them for their lack of faith and their stubborn refusal to believe those who had seen him after he had risen. He said to them, 'Go into all the world and preach the gospel to all creation. Whoever believes and is baptised will be saved, but whoever does not believe will be condemned. And these signs will accompany those who believe: in my name they will drive out demons; they will speak in new tongues; they will pick up snakes with their hands; and when they drink deadly poison, it will not hurt them at all; they will place their hands on people who are ill, and they will get well.' After the Lord Jesus had spoken to them, he was taken up into heaven and he sat at the right hand of God. Then the disciples went out and preached everywhere, and the Lord worked with them and confirmed his word by the signs that accompanied it. (Mark 16:14-20)

Is it possible that, like many nuclear power corporations and like the Provisional Irish Republican Army, the Church has experienced momentous historical events that have caused a Great *Decommission* to take place and to be accepted, with regard to ministering the supernatural gifts of the Holy Spirit, including the gift of healing? I believe that this may indeed be the case, and so it is worthwhile reviewing mainstream Church history with a view to identifying such events and exposing them as impediments to, among other things, a successful healing ministry in the Church down through the ages to include the present time. The redemptive nature of the gospel means that, once these events have been identified, we have an opportunity to undo past mistakes through renunciation and repentance.

The Giver of the Gift

Since we have documented that the gift of healing is identified with a particular set of supernatural gifts administered by the Holy Spirit and it is, in the main, these supernatural gifts that are lacking in our churches, it is worthwhile examining the nature of the Giver. Orthodox theology tells us that He is a distinct person of the Trinity, co-equal with the Father and the Son, and is of the same substance. In affirming the Holy Spirit as a person independent of the Father and the Son, Dr Edward Henry Bickersteth in his seminal work on the Trinity states:

> Now if, altogether apart from this investigation, you had been asked to name those qualities which evidence personal existence, you would have been quite content to answer: Show me that

which has mind, and affection, and will, which can act, and speak, and direct . . . and that . . . must possess personality, or personality cannot exist.[176]

He goes on to show example after example of the personal attributes of the Holy Spirit, concluding with the following summary:

- He testifies with personal witness (Romans 8:16; Acts 5:32).

- He communicates with personal authorities (Acts 15:28).

- He invites with personal messengers (Revelation 22:17).

- He is personally present[177] in a sense in which Jesus is personally absent (John 16:7).

- He can be personally blasphemed (as Christ may be personally blasphemed) but only upon peril of eternal damnation (Matthew 12:31).

- He cries in our hearts '*Abba*, Father' (Galatians 4:6).

- *He can be vexed and grieved* (Isaiah 63:10; Ephesians 4:30).[178]

We will look at events and occasions in Church history as a result of which it is possible that the Holy Spirit may have been uniquely offended in relation to these supernatural gifts that He administers. We know that throughout the lifetime of the Church, including the present Church age, the Holy Spirit has continued to lead and guide,

---

176. Bickersteth, p.124.
177. This is His manifest presence as compared to His omnipresence.
178. Bickersteth, p.126.

to illuminate the Scriptures, to convict of sin, and to regenerate believing individuals so that they are 'born again'. The analysis that follows relates exclusively to the supernatural gifts that, we have contended, have not been *withdrawn*, but, due to our deliberate actions, may have been to a large degree *withheld*.

Some Events From Church History

Event #1

The first of these events occurred before the apostolic era had properly ended. John, who was an old man, had been exiled to the island of Patmos. Early Church tradition says that John was banished by the Roman authorities for refusing to acknowledge Caesar as a god. This tradition is plausible, since banishment was a common punishment used for a range of state offences during the times of Imperial Rome. During this period on one 'Lord's Day', John was worshipping and was given a series of visions from Jesus Christ, which he subsequently wrote down and which we now recognise as the last book in our Bibles, the Apocalypse or book of Revelation. The early part of the revelation deals with 'the seven churches in the province of Asia' (Revelation 1:4a) before revealing future events in apocalyptic language from chapter 4 onwards. In Revelation 3:20, we have one of the most famous 'evangelistic' verses in the Bible. Famous paintings and evangelistic appeals portray the risen Jesus desiring, but not forcing, entrance into our lives. This message is true, and many people have responded to it with eternal consequences. The original context of the verse, however, written as part of a short letter to one of seven churches in the region and identified by the writer, is 'What the *Spirit* says to the churches' (Revelation 3:22b, emphasis added). This particular church at Laodicea had become so self-sufficient that it was no longer relying on the Spirit of the living God. The One whom John in his earlier writings described as the 'Advocate, the Holy Spirit, whom the Father will send in my name' (John 14:26a) had seemingly been evicted from this ancient church body – how then could it be true to these words of Jesus: '[They] will do the works I have been doing, and they will do even greater things than these, because I am going to the Father' (John 14:12b)? A large proportion of Bible commentators regard the seven letters to the seven churches as warnings to the Church down through the ages. If we are to be effective in Spirit-enabled ministries such as miraculous healing, then we, as the Church – locally, denominationally and universally – must repent of our proneness to self-sufficiency.

Event #2

The second event is the 2nd-century rise of Montanism, later regarded as heretical.

> The chief sources for the history of the movement are Eusebius' *Historia ecclesiastica* (Ecclesiastical History), the writings of Tertullian and Epiphanius, and inscriptions, particularly those in central Phrygia.

> According to the known history, Montanus, a then recent Christian convert, appeared at Ardabau, a small village in Phrygia, about 156. He fell into a trance and began to 'prophesy under the influence of the Spirit.' He was soon joined by two

young women, Prisca, or Priscilla, and Maximilla, who also began to prophesy. The movement spread throughout Asia Minor. Inscriptions have indicated that a number of towns were almost completely converted to Montanism. After the first enthusiasm had waned, however, the followers of Montanus were found predominantly in the rural districts.[179]

The message of Montanism was that the Paraclete, the Holy Spirit, whom Jesus is recorded as having promised in John 14:26a, was revealing Himself to the world through the movement's founder, Montanus, together with his female cohorts. At first, this possibility did not seem to be contrary to the doctrines of the Church or to attack the authority of the primitive Church hierarchy. It seems from the writings of the time that the Church acknowledged the charismatic gift of prophecy[180] and held it in esteem.

It soon became clear, however, that the Montanist prophecy was new. True prophets did not, as Montanus did, deliberately induce a kind of ecstatic intensity and a state of passivity and then maintain that the words they spoke were the voice of the Spirit. It also became clear that the claim of Montanus to have the final revelation of the Holy Spirit implied that something could be added to the teaching of Christ and the apostles and that, therefore, the Church had to accept a fuller revelation.

---

179. 'Montanism', written by the Editors of *Encyclopaedia Britannica*.
180. Which evidently had not disappeared upon the death of the last of the apostles.

When it became obvious that the Montanist doctrine was an attack on the Catholic faith, the bishops of Asia Minor gathered in synods and finally excommunicated the Montanists, probably *c.* 177. Montanism then became a separate sect with its seat of government at Pepuza. It maintained the ordinary Christian ministry but imposed on it higher orders of patriarchs and associates who were probably successors of the first Montanist prophets. It continued in the East until severe legislation against Montanism by Emperor Justinian I (reigned 527–565) essentially destroyed it, but some remnants evidently survived into the 9th century.[181]

Despite the fact that entire Christian communities in Asia Minor had taken the 'New Prophecy' as genuine and that Tertullian, one of the most significant and influential Church Fathers, was an overt supporter, the Church did not countenance the authenticity of Montanism.

Instead, there came to be a vehement emphasis on the ending of the age of miracle and revelation now that the last of the twelve apostles was dead. To Iraneus, the normal ministry of word and sacrament is in principle the point where the Spirit of God is encountered, not at emotional ecstasies which reject rationality and tradition. Anti-Montanist reaction reinforced the belief that the apostolic canon is closed; but it did nothing to diminish millenarian hopes which long retained orthodox defenders [of Montanism].[182]

---

181. Written by the Editors of *Encyclopaedia Britannica*.
182. McManners, p.30, quoting Chadwick.

The emergence of Montanism naturally hastened the fixing of the New Testament canon of Scripture in a form substantially as we now know it.

Tertullian had coined the terminology which was to dominate Western theology – Trinitas: 'Three persons in one substance'; and of Christ: 'Two substances or natures in one person'. Around the same time as the rise of Montanism, a priest named Praxeas had come from Asia Minor and had advocated an opposition to the distinctions that Justin had earlier made between the Father, as God transcendent, and the Son, as God immanent. He had also challenged the authenticity of the Montanist prophecy. In his tract *Against Praxeas* Tertullian alleged that in his denial of the Trinity, Praxeas had 'put to flight the Paraclete and crucified the Father'.

What if the Paraclete had indeed been in some measure put to flight at that period in Church history? But not because the Montanist prophecy was wholly authentic, but because His supernatural gifting had been spurned! Roger E. Elson stumbles upon this possibility (in a book aimed at identifying the common ground that authenticates Christian belief as either orthodox or heretical) when he says:

> This 'New Prophecy' movement (as it [Montanism] was known in the second century) posed a serious challenge to the stability of Christianity ...because of the claim that one man's prophecies were equal to the apostles' teaching and writings. *Unfortunately, the official church leaders may have overreacted to Montanism. It appears that the reaction against it inadvertently led to a*

decrease and eventual cessation of the gifts of the Spirit among Christians. (Emphasis added)[183]

What an admission!

Subsequently, Montanism appears to have flourished in the West, principally in Carthage under the leadership of Tertullian in the 3rd century. As previously cited, it had almost died out in the 5th and 6th centuries, although some evidence indicates that it survived into the 9th century.

Event #3

During the 4th century when the Apostles' Creed[184] was introduced into circulation (and this is respectfully stated), it appeared that the Third Person of the Trinity had been relegated to same level as the Church that He had founded, together with several of its key doctrines:

> I believe in God, the Father Almighty,
> Maker of heaven and earth.
> And in Jesus Christ, his only Son, our Lord,
> Who was conceived by the Holy Ghost, born of the Virgin Mary,
> Suffered under Pontius Pilate, was crucified, dead, and buried;
> He descended to hell.
> The third day he rose again from the dead.
> He ascended to heaven and sitteth on the right hand

---

183 Olson, Roger E., *The Mosaic of Christian Belief* (Intervarsity Press, 2002) p.59

184. 'This creed is called the Apostles' Creed not because it was produced by the apostles themselves but because it contains a brief summary of their teachings. It sets forth their doctrine "in sublime simplicity, in unsurpassable brevity, in beautiful order, and with liturgical solemnity". In its present form it is dated no later than the 4th century. More than any other Christian creed, it may justly be called an ecumenical symbol of faith. This translation of the Latin text was approved by the CRC Synod of 1988.' 'Apostles' Creed', Christian Reformed Church, https://new.crcna.org/welcome/beliefs/creeds/apostles-creed (accessed 3 October 2021).

of God the Father Almighty.
From thence he shall come to judge the quick and
the dead.
I believe in the Holy Ghost,
The Holy Catholic[185] *Church,*
The communion of saints,
The forgiveness of sins,
The resurrection of the body,
And the life everlasting.
Amen. (Emphasis added)

Event #4

A significant opportunity emerged to heal the offence
of the 2nd century in our third noted event from Church
history. This involved a dispute between the Eastern and
Western churches relating to the procession of the Holy
Spirit, which emerged as early as AD 411[186] and finally
resulted in the Great Schism between East and West in
1054. This event, known as the Filioque (from the Latin,
meaning 'and from the son'), involved the controversy as
to whether the Holy Spirit proceeds from the Father only,
or from both the Father and the Son. We see stated in John
15:26-27 that the Holy Spirit proceeds from the Father
'When the Advocate comes, whom I will send to you from
the Father – the Spirit of truth *who goes out from the*
Father – he will testify about me. And you also must testify,
for you have been with me from the beginning' (emphasis
added). This was the position taken by the Eastern churches
and is reflected in the earliest version of the Nicene Creed
which states, 'I believe in the Holy Spirit, the Lord, the

---

185. That is, the true Christian church of all times and all places.
186. Price, Richard, and Gaddis, Michael, eds, *The Acts of the Council of Chalcedon*
     (Liverpool: Liverpool University Press, 2005), p.193: 'We acknowledge the living and
     holy Spirit, the living Paraclete, who [is] from the Father and the Son.'

Giver of life, who proceeds from the Father'. However, support for the Holy Spirit also proceeding from the Son comes from John 16:7, 'But very truly I tell you, it is for your good that I am going away. Unless I go away, the Advocate will not come to you; but if I go, *I will send him to you*' (emphasis added).

This was the position taken by the Western churches and the offending 'and the Son' statement was added to the Nicene Creed as evidenced by later Western versions: 'I believe in the Holy Spirit, the Lord, the Giver of life, who proceeds from the Father and the Son'. Later Eastern versions add the word 'only': 'I believe in the Holy Spirit, the Lord, the Giver of life, who proceeds from the Father only'. Our understanding of the procession is further confused by Galatians 4:6: 'Because you are his sons, God sent the Spirit of his Son into our hearts, the Spirit who calls out, *"Abba*, Father."'

The procession of the Holy Spirit upon the Church, surely a major cause for rejoicing, instead became the primary reason for a major split in the Church. Psalm 133 is often quoted in the context of Christian unity:

> How good and pleasant it is when God's people live together in unity!
>
> It is like precious oil poured on the head, running down on the beard, running down on Aaron's beard, down on the collar of his robe. It is as if the dew of Hermon were falling on Mount Zion. For there the LORD bestows his blessing, even life for evermore.

Rather than the unity that welcomes the presence and ministry of the Holy Spirit, the Filioque controversy caused a disunity in the Church that has never been healed in a period of almost a millennium!

Event #5

The fifth event is regarded by many as the most significant one in Church history since Pentecost: the Protestant Reformation. The Reformation began as a renewal movement within the established Roman Catholic Church of the 16th century. Luther is given the publicity as being the champion of the movement but there were many in Europe who were challenged by what they regarded as the hypocrisy of the contemporary Church, who questioned the authenticity of its doctrine based on tradition and who opposed the power of the hierarchy.

We are indebted to the Reformers for 'rediscovering' salvation by grace through faith, establishing the priesthood of all believers and exposing the corruption in the machinery of the Church, such as the sale of indulgences. However, when new articles of faith emerged from the movement, references to the gifts of the Holy Spirit were practically absent. While we have previously made mention of an incident whereby Luther himself was credited with the gift of healing, and there was the report of miraculous events among the Moravians in the post-Reformation era, the working of miracles was under-emphasised by the Reformers. This phenomenon was part of an overall tendency by the Reformers to overcompensate[187] in all of

---

187. The most divisive overcompensation, even among Protestant denominations, is the works versus faith argument. Luther's emphasis was that salvation was by grace alone through faith alone. However, if the act of exercising faith is the free choice of the Christian, this could be construed as a work and therefore salvation would not be of grace. Long story short, in the formulation of Reformed theology, the result was the doctrine of unconditional election, whereby the elect person, unable to exercise faith because of that person's sinful state, is saved by God's grace *before* exercising faith (which is a post-conversion gift).

the areas of the doctrine of Rome that they were most opposed to. For example, the statues and adornments were considered to be idolatrous and, as a result, Reformation buildings were dull and unadorned and hence uninviting. The confessional was disregarded as being unnecessary for absolution of sin in light of the rediscovery by Luther of 'the Priesthood of all Believers'. Consequently, the Church lost the capacity for confession for accountability as James 5:16 encourages: 'Therefore confess your sins to each other and pray for each other so that you may be healed.' The power of this kind of confession has only been rediscovered by Protestant denominations in the past few decades.

We have already touched on the fact that Reformed theology places such an emphasis on the sovereignty of God that it finds it difficult to come to terms with divine interventions such as healing. Perhaps the second and third generation Reformers, who had had more time to consider their major doctrinal disagreements with Rome and formulate what would become Reformed theology had, like many others, misunderstood the sovereignty of God in the context of time as opposed to eternity. We humans are creatures of time and it is impossible for us to properly contemplate eternity. Is it possible that the Reformers' concept of the sovereignty of God was like Shakespeare, having written, say, *All's Well that Ends Well*, directing it and watching it being performed for the first time, knowing the content and the characters, he knows how it should play out, because he is directing it, he knows that the performance will stick exactly to the script? So, he is somehow predestining the performance of the play. If this is the concept, it is a poor analogy since it paints a picture of God as being subject to time, having to wait for a series of consecutive events to take place, albeit by His unchangeable direction, before the *advent* of 'eternity'. It is equally deficient to portray the concept of eternity as a never-ending timeline. It is still grossly inadequate as an illustration, but it is more satisfactory to regard the sovereignty of God as being more like one having a panoramic view of say a racetrack or endurance course, and seeing the whole route from start to finish, and everything in between, all at once. Being outside of it, but being able to intervene if some of the competitors begin to tire, are injured or are discouraged; seeing who has finished the course, who is presently on the track and who is yet to start. It must be emphasised, it is still grossly inadequate as an illustration, but it promotes the idea of God intervening miraculously through the gift of healing without undermining His sovereignty.

In the context of miracles such as healing, it has long been the practice[188] of the Roman Catholic Church to venerate holy people after their death through beatification and sainthood. For an individual to be canonised as a saint, in addition to a verified pious life, he or she has to have had miracles credited to him or her. Whether something is indeed a miracle is judged by the Vatican beatification tribunal of the Congregation of the Causes of Saints, which consists of eight Roman doctors and twenty-five cardinals and bishops and their staff. Their job, in essence, is to determine scientifically whether medical miracles are indeed miracles.

---

188. Due to the concern that the veneration of saints might threaten the worship of Jesus, the Second Council of Nicaea in 787 declared that God alone could be worshipped and saints were given respect.

Sara Kettler writes in a web article[189] how two separate miracles of healing were credited to Mother Teresa which made it possible, nine years after her death, for her to be canonised as Saint Teresa of Calcutta. The first of these involved the healing of a woman with a lump in her abdomen.

> In 1998, Monica Besra went to a Missionaries of Charity home in West Bengal, India, as she had a fever, headaches, vomiting, and swollen stomach. She had begun treatment for tuberculous meningitis the year before. However, the medications she'd taken – intermittently, depending on what her family could afford – hadn't kept a lump from growing in her abdomen (though some reports have described Besra as suffering from cancerous tumors, the growth could have been caused by tuberculosis). Surgery was considered to be necessary, however Besra was too weak and unwell to undergo an operation. On 5 September 1998 Besra was praying in the Missionaries of Charity chapel when she saw a light emanating from a photo of Mother Teresa. Later, a medallion that had touched Mother Teresa's body was placed on Besra's abdomen, and a sister said a prayer while asking Mother Teresa for help. Besra awoke early the next day to find her tumor had disappeared. Medical exams showed the abdominal mass was no longer there, and the doctors she'd seen agreed Besra no longer required surgery.

189. Sara Kettler, 'Mother Teresa: The Miracles That Made Her a Saint', Biography (updated 14 October 2020), https://www.biography.com/news/mother-teresa-miracles-saint (accessed 3 October 2021).

The theologians and medical experts who delved into the case found there was no earthly explanation for Besra's recovery. Her cure was therefore attributed to the miraculous intervention of Mother Teresa. This miracle was recognised by the Vatican in 2002. The second healing miracle documented by Kettler involved the healing of a man with brain abscesses:

> In 2008, Brazilian Marcilio Haddad Andrino was close to death. An infection had left his brain with abscesses and accumulating fluid, and his worsening condition made him fall into a coma. His wife, Fernanda, prayed to Mother Teresa for help. A priest gave Fernanda a relic of Mother Teresa when the couple got married and she 'put the relic on Marcilio's head, where he had the abscesses. I recited the prayer of beatification and also what came from my heart'.

> In a last-ditch effort to save his life, he was sent into surgery to drain the fluid around his brain. But before the operation could begin, Andrino miraculously woke up and asked, 'What am I doing here?' His wife's prayers were answered as Andrino made a fast and complete recovery. The abscesses and fluid around his brain disappeared without the need for surgery. (In addition, though the drugs he'd taken were thought to have rendered him infertile, Andrino and his wife went on to have children.)

> As before, the Congregation for the Causes of Saints and a medical committee examined the case. No medical explanation was discovered

for how Andrino had been cured. In 2015, his recovery was deemed to be Mother Teresa's second miracle. Pope Francis recognised this in December of that year.

In addition to healing miracles, saints down through the ages have been accredited with miracles of levitation, producing fire from their fingertips and communicating with animals. A late 5th-century text established the popular tale of 3rd-century martyr St Denis carrying his own decapitated head post-execution. Of course, more recent phenomena such as stigmata and weeping statues are in the same category as historic miracle healing claims, and so the tradition continues.

There is the danger of idolatry and superstition in accepting the processes described above and it was this that the Reformers rightly wanted to steer clear of. Did they inadvertently perpetuate a quenching of the healing ministry of the Holy Spirit in the process?

Event #6

The sixth significant historical event is the Asuza Street Revival. The origin of the modern Pentecostal movement is traced back to Los Angeles and the Azusa Street Revival, whose meetings ran from 1906–1915 and which began when Holiness preacher William J. Seymour witnessed seven men, with whom he had been praying, spontaneously beginning to speak in tongues. This was obviously a very uncommon occurrence, and it attracted a large crowd interested in witnessing and experiencing what is biblically referred to as the baptism of, or baptism in, the Holy Spirit. Many received this baptism, of which Pentecostals believe speaking in tongues is the evidence; many came to faith in Jesus Christ and it is claimed that many more received miraculous healings. The Holiness Movement to which Seymour belonged typically holds to a second blessing theology: that sanctification is an event rather than a process, resulting in the Christian attaining a state of holiness through a post-conversion work of grace. This belief grew out of Methodism and is embraced by Church of the Nazarene and Salvation Army denominations. Seymour's mentor, Charles Parham, believed in a third blessing, the baptism of the Holy Spirit, and although Seymour believed in this experience and preached on the subject, he did not receive the baptism himself until some days into the revival.

In an age of intense racial segregation in the United States of America, it was surprising that all nationalities[190] (Seymour was himself African-American, the son of an emancipated slave) and classes participated in the meetings. Women also participated in the leadership, which was noteworthy, considering women in the US were not permitted to vote until 1920! Many 'non-Holiness' denominations were also represented, including Baptists, Presbyterians and Mennonites.

Among first-hand accounts were reports of the blind having their sight restored, diseases cured instantly, and immigrants whose languages were German, Yiddish and Spanish all being spoken to in their native language by uneducated black members, who translated the languages into English through a supernatural ability.

---

190. It is alleged that, in September 1906, a Los Angeles newspaper had described the happenings at the meetings as 'a disgraceful intermingling of the races ...'

Christians from many traditions were critical, saying the movement was hyper-emotional, involved the misuse of Scripture and neglected focus on Christ by overemphasising the Holy Spirit. Within a short time, ministers were warning their congregations to stay away from the Azusa Street Mission. Some called the police and tried to get the building shut down.[191] Once again the ministry and the gifting of the Holy Spirit was undermined by 'traditional' Christianity.

Interestingly, while many of the mainstream denominations are in decline, the Pentecostal movement presently claims to be one of the fastest growing traditions in world Christianity.[192]

Event #7

The final and most recent event that the author wants to consider is the advent of the modern Charismatic Movement. Pentecostalism continued in its denominational form for half a century. By the mid-1950s, however, interdenominational healing revivals were becoming widespread in the US, leading to a broader acceptance among mainstream denominations of Pentecostal gifts and, in particular, the possibility of miraculous healing. By the 1960s, many of the teachings of Pentecostalism were finding acceptance among Christians

---

191. Synan, Vinson, *The Century of the Holy Spirit: 100 years of Pentecostal and Charismatic Renewal, 1901–2001* (Nashville, TN: Thomas Nelson, 2001), pp.42-45.

192. Zurlo, Gina A., Johnson, Todd, M. and Crossing, Peter F., 'World Christianity and Mission 2021: Questions About the Future', *International Bulletin of Mission Research,* vol. 45, no. 1 (January 2021), pp. 15-25, https://journals.sagepub.com/doi/full/10.1177/2396939320966220 (accessed 19 August 2022): 'The Pentecostal/Charismatic movement is one of the fastest-growing trends in World Christianity today, and it has been for some time. This movement grew from 58 million in 1970 to 656 million in 2021. The Global South is home to 86 percent of all Pentecostals/Charismatics in the world', p.18.

within mainstream Protestant denominations. Dennis Bennett was an Episcopal rector who had received what he had regarded as the baptism of the Holy Spirit in early 1960 and had begun to teach the reality of his experience to his congregation, with the result that they began to receive this experience also. This led to criticism and controversy among church hierarchy and laity alike; however, meetings where speaking in tongues and healing, which included praying over the sick and anointing with oil, became a more common and widespread occurrence in mainstream Protestant congregations, including Lutherans and Presbyterians. Unlike the earlier Pentecostal revival, the Charismatic Movement gained traction within denominations. Interestingly, the authenticity of this new wave was not recognised by mainstream Pentecostalism for several decades, and the corresponding gifts were initially considered to be counterfeit. This was particularly the case when, in the late 1960s, the Catholic Charismatic Renewal began. Methodists became involved in the movement in the 1970s. The geographical spread of the Charismatic Movement from the US was mainstream denomination based.

Books such as *Chasing the Dragon* by Jackie Pullinger and *The Cross and the Switchblade* by David Wilkerson were greatly influential among mainstream denominations in encouraging individuals to seek a greater dependence upon the Holy Spirit in ministry and in everyday living.

Eventually, the Evangelical denominations began to embrace the Charismatic gifts. However, in many instances there was an emphasis on a 'fullness of the Spirit' for those church groupings whose articles of faith did not encourage the acceptance of a post-conversion baptism of the Spirit. The original Greek text in Ephesians 5:18, translated 'Do not get drunk on wine . . . instead be filled with the Spirit', is in the present continuous tense, 'Keep on being filled with the Holy Spirit'.[193] So, just as a Holiness Movement that emphasised a post-conversion sanctification (second blessing) event birthed a Pentecostal movement that emphasised a post-conversion Holy Spirit event, Evangelicals who regarded sanctification as a post-conversion process rather than an event were more likely to regard the receiving of the Holy Spirit as an ongoing filling process rather than an event. This 'fullness' process also played down the inevitable 'two-tier' aspect of being a Christian (those having had 'The Baptism' and those who hadn't) together with the emphasis on speaking in tongues as the 'initial evidence'.

C. Peter Wagner, who is cited earlier in this work in a different context, referred to a 1980s movement as the Third Wave of the Holy Spirit,[194] which expressed itself through the formation of churches and denomination-like organisations. These groups he refers to as 'neo-charismatic' and are distinct from the Charismatic Movement of the historic mainstream churches, citing the Vineyard Movement founded by the late John Wimber as typical.

And so, once again, came the division and the corresponding potential offence. What should have been a renewal movement uniting a wide variety of mainstream Christian

193. Or more accurately, the present continuous tense in the passive voice: 'Keep on allowing yourselves to be filled with the Holy Spirit.'
194. Wagner, C. Peter, *The Third Wave of the Holy Spirit: Encountering the Power of Signs and Wonders Today* (Ann Arbor, MI: Servant Publications Vine Books, 1988).

denominations through a shared experience of the Holy Spirit resulted in the production of a variety and succession of super-church movements.

Both the Pentecostal Revival and the Charismatic Movement provided the spiritual seedbed for the flourishing of the supernatural gifts, including healing, to the whole Church. Unfortunately, the unity was not there. Psalm 133, previously quoted in the context of Christian unity, and rightly so, although written a millennium before the birth of the Church, emphasises the principle of brothers (and sisters) dwelling in unity. The application almost always relates to the fact that 'there the LORD commands a blessing'. That blessing, according to the psalmist, is 'life for evermore' and so we can conclude that Christian unity encourages faith that leads to people receiving everlasting life, that is, salvation. What is generally missed is an emphasis on the preceding verses:

> It is like the precious oil poured on the head, running on the beard, down on Aaron's beard, down on the collar of his robe. It is as if the dew of Hermon were falling on Mount Zion. (Psalm 133:2)

This oil seems to speak of the Holy Spirit, and of a rich and plentiful anointing upon a 'kingdom of priests'. This dew reminds us of the refreshing and revival brought about by that Holy Spirit. One fundamental key to the ministry of the Holy Spirit is Christian unity. It was a condition met by the early Christians in those few days between Ascension and Pentecost when they were 'all together in one place' (Acts 2:1).

Renunciation and Repentance

The prophet Daniel understood from the Scriptures that the desolation of Jerusalem would last seventy years before the exiled people would return, and then the land would be restored. He knew that God is sovereign, and yet he felt the need to plead with and petition God with fasting, in sackcloth and ashes, to bring this restoration about. Moreover, he confessed the sins of his people (Daniel 9:4-19). Should we consider whether there is a lesson, or a series of lessons, from Church history regarding the present, apparent relative failure of the Church's healing ministry, and if there is a Daniel-like confession that Church leaders and individual members need to make to recommission us as agents of supernatural healing?

The author has sought God over a protracted period of time in considering the prayer that follows. It addresses simply those major events in Church history, outlined above, where it is possible that we have offended the Holy Spirit, particularly in the realm of the supernatural gifts that He has been pleased to bestow on the Church through the promise of Jesus. The author has prayed this prayer himself and it is also his prayer that heads of denominations, local church leaders, pastors, elders, church officers and Christians generally would join the author in repentance.

Humbling ourselves before the Lord is never a waste of time. 'Humble yourselves before the Lord, and he will lift you up' (James 4:10).

Prayer

Holy Spirit, we regret having vexed and grieved You, having failed to discern Your genuine works from counterfeit works and works of the flesh.

We repent of our proneness to self-sufficiency that has rendered You superfluous to much of our activity as a Church.

Through our emphasis on rationality and tradition, we have restricted our encounter with You to the ministry of 'word and sacrament'; we have effectively relegated Your status within the Trinity and we are sorry.

We rejoice in Your procession upon the Church.

We reject idolatry and superstition, but repent of actions where this rejection has inadvertently led to a quenching of Your healing ministry.

We confess that we have perpetuated division through competition and denominationalism, which has contravened the spirit of the high-priestly prayer of the Lord Jesus and has restricted the flow of Your anointing oil and the dropping down of Your refreshing dew.

Amen
And Amen!

Bibliography

Anderson, Neil T., *Released From Bondage* (Tunbridge Wells: Monarch, 1993)

Barnett, Paul, *The Message of 2 Corinthians* (Leicester: IVP, 1988)

Bennett, Rita, *Emotionally Free* (Eastbourne: Kingsway, 1982)

Bennett, Rita, *How to Pray for Inner Healing* (Eastbourne: Kingsway, 1984)

Bennett, Rita, *Making Peace With Your Inner Child* (Eastbourne: Kingsway, 1987)

Berkof, L., *Systematic Theology* (London: Banner of Truth, 1958)

Bickersteth, Edward Henry, *The Trinity* (Grand Rapids, MI: Kregal Publications, 1957)

Bingham, Rowland V., *The Bible and the Body* (Toronto: Evangelical Publishers, 1921)

Bonnke, Reinhard, *Evangelism By Fire* (Frankfurt: Christ for all Nations, 1999)

Bounds, E.M., *Power Through Prayer* (Grand Rapids, MI: Baker, 1978)

Brown, Paul E., *Jesus: The Hidden Years* (Leominster: Day One Publications, 2017)

Carson, Herbert, *Spiritual Gifts for Today?* (Eastbourne: Kingsway, 1987)

Chadwick, Owen, *The Reformation* (Harmondsworth: Penguin, 1972)

Cole, R. Alan, *Galatians, Tyndale New Testament Commentaries* (Leicester: IVP, 1984)

Cross, F.L., ed., *The Oxford Dictionary of the Christian Church* (Oxford: Oxford University Press, 1983)

Dickinson, Robert, *God Does Heal Today* (Carlisle: Paternoster, 1995)

Douglas, Alban, *God's Answers to Man's Questions* (Greenville, SC: W.D. Kennedy, 1981)

Dowley, Tim, ed., *The History of Christianity* (Oxford: Lion, 1990)

Elton, G.R., *Reformation Europe, 1517–1559* (London: Fontana, 1969)

Elwell, W.A., ed., *Evangelical Dictionary of Theology* (Carlisle: Paternoster, 1995)

Epp, Theodore H., *James: The Epistle of Applied Christianity* (Lincoln, NE: Back to the Bible, 1980)

Estep, William R., *Renaissance and Reformation* (Grand Rapids, MI: Eerdmans, 1992)

Evans, Craig A., and Porter, Stanley E., eds, *Dictionary of New Testament Background* (Leicester: IVP, 2000)

Fitch, William, *God and Evil: Studies in the Mystery of Suffering and Pain* (London: Pickering & Inglis, 1967)

Foot, David R.P., *Divine Healing in the Scriptures* (Worthing: Henry E. Walter, 1969)

Gaebelein, A.C., *The Healing Question* (New York, NY: Our Hope, 1925)

Gross, Edward N., *Miracles, Demons and Spiritual Warfare* (Grand Rapids, MI: Baker, 1990)

Guy, Laurie, *Introducing Early Christianity* (Downers Grove, IL: IVP, 2004)

Grosheide, F.W., *The New International Commentary on the New Testament* (Grand Rapids, MI: Eerdmans, 1976)

Hafemann, S.J., 'Suffering', in *Dictionary of Paul and His Letters* (eds Gerald F. Hawthorne and Ralph P. Martin; Leicester: IVP, 1993)

Hibbert, Albert, *Smith Wigglesworth: The Secret of his Power* (Shippensburg, PA: Destiny Image, 1987)

Hillerbrand, H.J., *The Oxford Encyclopaedia of the Reformation,* vol. 3 (Oxford: Oxford University Press, 1992)

Hinn, Benny, *This Is Your Day for a Miracle* (Milton Keynes: Nelson Word, 1996)

Hylson-Smith, Kenneth, *The Churches in England from Elizabeth I to Elizabeth II, Vol. 2: 1689–1833* (London: SCM Press, 1997)

Idle, Christopher, *The Journal of John Wesley* (Oxford: Lion, 2003)

Johnson, Bill, *When Heaven Invades Earth* (Shippensburg, PA: Destiny Image, 2003)

Kendall, R.T., *The Thorn in the Flesh* (London: Hodder & Stoughton, 1999)

Kendrick, Graham A., *The Source* (Bury St Edmunds: Kevin Mayhew, 1998)

Kuhlman, Kathryn, *Nothing Is Impossible with God* (Englewood Cliffs, NJ: Prentice-Hall, 1974)

Lane, A.N.S., *The Lion Concise Book of Christian Thought* (Tring: Lion, 1984)

Lawrence, Roy, *Invitation to Healing* (Eastbourne: Kingsway, 1979)

Leman, Kevin and Carlson, Randy, *Unlocking the Secrets of Your Childhood Memories* (Eastbourne: Monarch, 1985)

Lewis, C.S., *The Screwtape Letters* (London: Fontana, 1955)

McCrossan, T.J. (re-edited Hicks, R. and Hagin, K.), *Bodily Healing and the Atonement* (New York, NY: Faith Library, 1982)

McManners, John, ed., *The Oxford Illustrated History of Christianity* (Oxford: Oxford University Press, 1992)

MacNutt, Francis, *The Prayer That Heals* (London: Hodder & Stoughton, 1988)

Madden, Peter J., *The Wigglesworth Standard: The Standard for God's End-time Army (Springdale, PA: Whitaker* House, 1993)

Manwaring, Paul, *Kisses From a Good God* (Shippensburg, PA: Destiny Image, 2012)

Martin, Ralph P., *1 and 2 Corinthians and Galatians* (London: Scripture Union, 1968)

Masters, Peter, *The Healing Epidemic* (London: Wakeman, 1988)

Morris, Leon, *The Apostolic Teaching of the Cross* (Grand Rapids, MI: Eerdmans 1955)

Newman, Richard, and Burkett, Randall K., *Black Apostles: Afro-American Clergy Confront the Twentieth Century* (Boston, MA: G.K. Hall & Co., 1978)

Nolen, William, *Healing: A Doctor in Search of a Miracle* (New York, NY: Random House, 1974)

Olson, Roger E., *The Mosaic of Christian Belief* (Downers Grove, IL: IVP, 2002)

Penn-Lewis, Jessie, with Roberts, Evan, *War On the Saints* (New York, NY: Thomas E. Lowe, Ltd, 1984)

Price, Richard, and Gaddis, Michael, eds, *The Acts of the Council of Chalcedon* (Liverpool: Liverpool University Press, 2005)

Ryrie, Charles Caldwell, *The Ryrie Study Bible: NASB* (Chicago, IL: Moody, 1976)

Synan, Vinson, *The Century of the Holy Spirit: 100 years of Pentecostal and Charismatic Renewal, 1901–2001* (Nashville, TN: Thomas Nelson, 2001)

Tasker, R.V.G., *2 Corinthians,* Tyndale New Testament Commentaries (Leicester: IVP, 1983)

Thomas, Keith, *Religion and the Decline of Magic* (Harmondsworth: Penguin, 1973)

Townsend, Anne J., *Prayer Without Pretending* (London: Scripture Union, 1977)

Unger, Merrill F., *The Baptism and Gifts of the Holy Spirit* (Chicago, IL: Moody, 1974)

Urquhart, Colin, *Anything You Ask* (London: Hodder & Stoughton, 1989)

Vos, Howard F., *Galatians: A Call to Christian Liberty* (Columbus, OH: Lutheran Book Concern, 1937)

Wagner, C. Peter, *How to Have a Healing Ministry Without Making Your Church Sick* (Ventura, CA: Regal Books, 1988)

Wagner, C. Peter, *The Third Wave of the Holy Spirit: Encountering the Power of Signs and Wonders Today* (Ann Arbor, MI: Servant Publications Vine Books, 1988)

Wagner, C. Peter, *Warfare Prayer* (Tunbridge Wells: Monarch, 1992)

Warrington, Keith, *Jesus the Healer: Paradigm or Unique Phenomenon?* (Carlisle: Paternoster, 2000)

White, Andrew Dickson, *A History of the Warfare of Science With Theology in Christendom* (Whitefish, MT: Kessinger, 2004)

Wigglesworth, Smith, *On Healing* (Springdale, PA: Whitaker House, 1999)

Wimber, John, *Power Evangelism: Signs and Wonders Today* (London: Hodder & Stoughton, 1985)

Wimber, John, *Power Healing* (London: Hodder & Stoughton, 1986)

Woolmer, John, *Healing and Deliverance* (London: Monarch, 1999)

Zurlo, Gina A., Johnson, Todd, M. and Crossing, Peter F., 'World Christianity and Mission 2021: Questions About the Future', *International Bulletin of Mission Research*, vol. 45, no. 1 (January 2021), pp. 15-25.